Archangels

Living Transmissions From the
Archangel of the Sun

*(Powerful Prayers to Saint Michael the Defender
of the Church)*

Angela Lewis

Published By **Zoe Lawson**

Angela Lewis

All Rights Reserved

Archangels: Living Transmissions From the Archangel of the Sun (Powerful Prayers to Saint Michael the Defender of the Church)

ISBN   978-1-77485-639-0

All rights reserved. No part of this guidebook shall be reproduced in any form without permission in writing from the publisher except in the case of brief quotations embodied in critical articles or reviews.

Legal & Disclaimer

The information contained in this ebook is not designed to replace or take the place of any form of medicine or professional medical advice. The information in this ebook has been provided for educational & entertainment purposes only.

The information contained in this book has been compiled from sources deemed reliable, and it is accurate to the best of the Author's knowledge; however, the Author cannot guarantee its accuracy and validity and cannot be held liable for any errors or omissions. Changes are periodically made to this book. You must consult your doctor or get professional medical advice before using any of the suggested remedies, techniques, or information in this book.

Upon using the information contained in this book, you agree to hold harmless the Author from and against any damages, costs, and expenses, including any legal fees potentially resulting from the application of any of the information provided by this guide. This disclaimer applies to any damages or injury caused by the use and application, whether directly or indirectly, of any advice or information presented, whether for breach of contract, tort, negligence, personal injury, criminal intent, or under any other cause of action.

You agree to accept all risks of using the information presented inside this book. You need to consult a professional medical practitioner in order to ensure you are both able and healthy enough to participate in this program.

TABLE OF CONTENTS

Chapter 1 Angels (And The Angelic Realm) 1

Chapter 2 Archangels The Heavenly, Magnificent Seven 6

Chapter 3 Spiritual Support Team Meeting 37

Chapter 4 Affirmation Ritual For Forgiveness 71

Chapter 5 Healing Through The Archangel Raphael 121

Chapter6 Roles And Capabilities Archangels 155

Chapter 1 Angels (and the Angelic Realm)

Are you familiar with the feeling of someone watching over you or hearing a whisper in your ear?

There are many who believe that humans walk the earth alone. Then there are those who recognize that we are surrounded every day by gentle, guiding partners. These gentle, guiding companions we call our angels. If you don't know them, I'd love to introduce you to them and provide tips for communicating with them.

The term "angel" can invoke many imagery. Some envision angels as sweet cherubs. Other imagine strong, winged beings equipped with swords. There are many types of angels, and each one serves a different purpose.

Many earth-walkers have difficulty understanding angels despite the visuals. They often confuse them and other spiritual beings. An angel by definition is a spiritual being that has never been on the earth. This means they were not born into animal or human flesh. The angels have not walked on the earth in the past. It will not do so in future. Their purpose, for all eternity, is to serve, protect and guide. Each of us carries special angels along with us wherever we go.

This is one reason I find angels fascinating. Although I believe it is my human perspective which makes it so I am amazed by their unconditional love. They are there at a moment's notice when we call. They are there to help us, as long it doesn't affect our divine or unfettered free will. They see beyond our flaws. There's nothing you can do to lose an angel's love or respect. There are few examples where love is so pure.

The angelic domain is where angels can be found. It's almost like a series if floors in the spiritual realm. It can be thought of as the angels' corporate headquarters. The seven-floors are where we communicate with the angels. There are also spiritual beings on lower floors. However, for some reason (such as having experienced a physical incarnation here on earth), they aren't considered true angels.

This book will provide an overview of the major players within the angelic realm, who can help support, protect and guide. We will focus mainly on the archangels (or guardian angels) and briefly discuss spirit guides. These spiritual beings are among the most intuitive and easy to connect with.

There are also other types of angels. However, it can be difficult to connect with them. It's not because they don't desire to communicate directly. It's just because communicating with us that way is not their job. Each angel and every level of an angel have a purpose. Nine levels of hierarchy are shared by the angels. You'll see that there are three tiers to this hierarchy. I will not go into detail about the tiers, as it is too confusing. It is still important to understand the various levels and personalities of angels, even though they are not active in your daily life.

* Seraphim is an angel of love.

Cherubim refer to angels of harmony as well as knowledge.

* Thrones represent angels of justice, peacemaking, and justice.

* Dominions represent angels of wisdom.

* Virtues, angels of wonders.

* Powers are angels that manifest in physical manifestations.

* Principalities are the Guardian Angels of the Earth.

* The archangels of God are angels who guide, protect and serve humanity.

* Guardian angels and angels are the angels who work most closely with humans every day.

As you can clearly see, there are many different types of angels serving various purposes. Each angel connects to different energies or personalities. This book will help you to learn how to be attuned to each of these energies. You can then become a more open channel for loving, angelic energy. I am thrilled for you to embark on this journey. I also know your angels feel the same. They've been waiting to meet you. They are not going to wait for you any longer.

Let me first introduce you to the seven great archangels.

Chapter 2 Archangels The Heavenly, Magnificent seven

Archangels spiritual beings are those who have a higher rank than angels. They are guardians, messengers, and angels. The bible lists seven holy angels. These are the ones we refer too as the archangels. According to heavenly rumours there may be more than seven but these are those that have been assigned for us on earth. These are the archangels to whom we have the closest, most intimate connection. I am going to briefly introduce these significant spirits of the spirit world.

The Archangels act as heavenly emissaries. They are master communicators who can show love, compassion, guidance and support us through our most difficult life situations. Each of these archangels acts as a channel between God or us. As the direct channel of communication between us, God or Goddess of our faith, we can think about them as such.

Archangels can be protective beings that remove negativity or dark energy from our lives.

The beauty in the archangels love us unconditionally. They see us, as beings in the light, and they guide us. They cannot see our failures, and they will not let us down. This does not mean we are incapable of making mistakes on earth and disappointing others. The archangels realize that these circumstances are challenges for our human spirit throughout the life we are living. They are obstacles to overcome in order to help the spirit grow or raise. The archangels are not harsh or cruel, but they will show love and compassion with their energy. They know that the suffering we endure on earth is enough.

It is important to show respect and gratitude to the archangels as you learn to communicate. The archangels understand that, while they have the power to summon their energies, they also serve as messengers and protective spirits. This is not an act worthy of worship. It is difficult to discern between actions that are angel worship or invoking and acknowledging the archangels. Do not confuse the two when you are referring to the Archangels.

Each of the archangels is given a name with a significant meaning. Let me give you a brief introduction to each.

Michael: Michael's Messenger

Michael's title translates to "Who's like God" in the realms archangels. Michael is considered the prince.

Michael is not only an angelic figure, but he also holds special significance for each one of us on earth. Michael has devoted his life to the security and well-being of our souls, using his powers of protection and light. His energy wraps around us like a protective blanket and shields us against all kinds of evil and negativity.

Michael is our spiritual ally, guiding us gently to God's will, and helping us to see God's intended design for each of our lives. He is an angel who will stand by you in times when it's hard to stay on track. His presence guides us towards the right decisions, and gives us the courage to take them.

Signs that Archangel Michael Is Present and Communicating With You

* Is this intuition or Michael? Did you ever hear your inner voice speak so loudly and insistently that it was impossible for you to ignore? Michael is your guide to the right direction.

* You feel it click. Do you ever feel that moment when everything suddenly makes sense and seems to click? Michael can be thanked for this.

* Fear is replaced by calm Fear is something that we all experience at some point in our

lives. Sometimes our safety and well-being are at stake. Other times elements in our lives have caused us to feel insecure, unstable, and uncertain about the future. Michael covers us with a sense security and calmness, even in our darkest hours.

* Indigo, blue and purple appear more frequently in your life. These colors are associated Michael. You might notice these colors more often than others. They might appeal to you, or you might catch a glimpse in your peripheral vision.

How to connect with Michael

At the chance of being redundant, i will repeat the same sentence for each of the archangels. The easiest way to communicate with the archangels, is to simply ask them for their help. This can often happen with our thoughts. There are situations when the strength of our emotions is sufficient for the archangels' to assist us. They will assist us in any situation where we are in need.

Still, it can strengthen your connection by participating in invoking ceremonies. The more we honor archangels energy, the higher our vibration will be and the closer we feel to them.

There is no right or incorrect way to connect with archangels. It's impossible to do it wrong. You will feel it if it feels right. Be open to it.

Here are some ways that you can connect with Michael if you enjoy the idea.

A prayer or invocation can be offered. This can be a written prayer, or you can just make one. Take into consideration the energies associated with the angel Michael you are seeking to connect. Begin by thanking God and acknowledging any divine intervention you have received. Your intention or need should be stated and Michael will help you. Invocations should end with gratitude. This puts your intent in the present, and not the future. You will be in a state where you wait. Close with your favorite blessings or prayers.

Light candles with Michael's color. Indigo, blue and purple are closely associated with Michael. Candles in these colors can be used to make connections with him. Protective candles such as those in shades of red or in white are good choices. Keep the candle lit while you focus on your purpose and needs.

God's Messenger Michael is a good communicator. I like to write down all my concerns, wishes, and intentions in a journal that I keep for Michael.

You will find the answers. Michael's messages are almost always simple. Listen to the voice within you and pay attention wherever it leads. Michael will provide guidance but you must first open yourself to receive it.

Raphael: Heavenly Healing Agent

Raphael represents the archangel for healing. He is the one who is always present for both the spiritual and physical bodies when they are in need of healing, recovery, and restoration. His name means, "God has overcome"/"God has healed". He embodies the energy required in healing, overcoming trials and despair.

You only need to ask Raphael to help you. Raphael will be there for you once your needs are expressed. Raphael will honor any request you make for his assistance.

Raphael can be present to each of us in our own ways, as we are all earthly beings. Because Raphael has our backs, he can see where we are in need of healing.

Raphael has been called many times for physical healing. Sometimes this happens in the form a true miracle. There are times when Raphael is called upon to heal us. We expect a certain result, and then we are disappointed. We need to realize that physical healing sometimes is not compatible with the direction the soul's travel. These are very difficult, difficult, and emotionally charged times. These times are when the spirit is really tested.

Raphael cannot change your course. Instead, he offers healing for the soul to help you feel at peace with your inner self.

Signs that Archangel Raphael has communicated and is present in you life

Raphael likes to make an impact visually to announce that he is there. Raphael's name might appear on more things, like street names and book covers. Or you may start to meet other people with this uncommon name. If Raphael shows you more angelic images, particularly those that contain green, this could be a sign that he is listening to what you have to say.

* Literally, higher vibrations Raphael, who is associated most strongly with healing, has a very powerful vibrational energies. It is possible to feel tingly when Raphael is around you. Raphael's kind of energy also produces heat. You might feel hot, hot or flushed when he is around.

* You will find all the information you are looking for right there. It can be hard for you to use your limited energy in healing. Raphael realizes that our internal voice can be difficult to hear, especially when it is distracted and worrying. Raphael communicates directly with you by putting the information in a place he knows you will find. You might find an article about your health on the Internet, or someone might help you locate the right doctor. Or you might browse the library's book giveaways and find a book you are interested in. These are all examples Raphael helping people heal by sharing knowledge.

* Shades rich and vibrant green. This is Raphael's color, and you may be more inclined to notice it in your environment when he is with you. Or, you may find that you have a greater appreciation of it in the natural environment. Perhaps you wander outside and see how the grass and leaves seem vibrant and almost glowing with life. This is Raphael.

How to connect Raphael

The only thing you need to do when speaking with any of the archangels is to ask for their assistance and guidance. They want to help, and they won't turn away from your in need just because they didn't like how you called. With this in mind, it's important to express gratitude for your presence. You can express gratitude verbally, through a gift, or mentally.

To make Raphael feel closer, we should focus on nature-healing rituals.

Find a quiet place and find a way to relax. Try to include green as much possible. A green blanket or robe is a good base. You can sit back and focus on the healing energy in your body. This is Raphael's energy. Allow him in. Let him flow through you, as he infuses healing energy into your body and spirit.

Raphael may be attracted by a ritual that includes lighting green candles, and anointing with an earthy oil. You can use chamomile and thyme as an oil for your anointing.

Raphael is available to help you if you are in need of physical healing.

To ensure safe travels, keep a little angel statue in your carry-on bag, wrapped in a piece if green cloth with a travelers prayer written on it.

Gabriel: Trumpet of Joy And Blessings

Gabriel almost always features a Horn. Gabriel is, like Michael and a messenger. He is however not the direct line between God or us. His power of communication may be a little different.

Gabriel rides ahead of us and announces the arrival. Gabriel is an archangel of protection and travel. The horn he carries can be used to create triumphant musical music. It is also used for announcing joy, jubilance, the blessings granted by wishes, and dreams coming true.

Gabriel is close to all women who have ever had a child in their womb. Gabriel is the archangel which protects and stays with unborn children throughout their pregnancy, as well as after birth. Gabriel is said by some to touch the baby's mouth just before birth in order to make him forget all the secrets and mysteries of heaven before he begins his earthly life. This is believed that it creates a small, sweet cleft in your upper lip. Gabriel's joyful trumpet announces unto the angels that another beautiful human being has been born.

Gabriel can also come when there's a need for truth. There are times in life when we make our own troubles because we refuse to see what is right in front of us. Gabriel is the one who blares his trumpet to force us to see what's really there. He has given us one of his gifts, the gift of clarity. Gabriel knows that clarity will help you forgive, grow, and continue living with love from your heart.

Signs that Archangel Gabriel is Communicating with You and Present in Your World

* You feel closer to the moon and her cycles. Gabriel is associated both with the feminine energies and the cyclical energy that the moon has. Each phase of the moon must be completed before it can become whole. Gabriel's energy is felt, and you can strengthen your relationship with him by making contact with the night sky or her celestial bodies.

* Gabriel likes to share his messages in dreams. The best time to receive heavenly

messages is while we're dreaming. Perhaps you woke up from a surreal dream or an experience that brought back a sense of reality or imagery. Gabriel may not always tell the whole story. Gabriel can only give you what you are looking for at the given moment. This is why you might remember certain parts of the dreams vividly while others may seem distant and impossible to reach.

* A predominant element or color is silver. Gabriel is associated in some way with silver. You may see twinkling silver sparks out of your eye or find an amazing number of silver coin on the ground during the day. Gabriel is your friend if you find a silver hooves.

Gabriel: How to connect

Gabriel's connection can feel very different from the one with the other angels. Gabriel is the most joyful among all the angels. Gabriel is your guide, but he also celebrates with you. If he's present, you may find yourself in a better mood or be more inclined to go to social gatherings. It could feel like you are bursting for joy. For the best connection with God, we should focus on rituals of happiness. Contentment, happiness, and beauty.

My favorite way to get in touch with Gabriel is to bathe myself in moonlight. Select a night that the moon is full, and the sky is clear. Make sure you are in a place free from distractions and quiet. You can then just sit. Just close your eyes, and the moon will bathe and energize you. This is not only a prayer for Gabriel but also a cleansing, restorative ritual. Call Gabriel and ask that Gabriel be at your side.

Next, imagine an angelic creature, surrounded only by a million twinkling Stars, coming towards your face. Feel his joyous energy. He will be glad to see you and you should thank him for his visit. You have two choices: either you can sit and watch your vision unfold, or you may express your need or wish. Listen for a moment to see if Gabriel gives any immediate answers. Sometimes, Gabriel may smile at us and surround us with his light.

Keep in touch with your gratitude. Recommend Gabriel to you.

Uriel: Angel for Wisdom and Motivation

Uriel, an archangel, represents wisdom, guidance and motivation. He is there for us when faced with a dilemma, a big decision or fork in the road. Uriel's name is "God IS my light" (or "fire of God"), and it is he that illuminates our path so we can see more clearly the direction we should take.

Uriel is also responsible for lighting a fire under our feet when we feel stuck or indifferent. Uriel is a wise person who can help us face difficult decisions. She also gives us the ability to believe in ourselves, which allows us to be courageous and move forward.

Before we can gain wisdom or move forward there must be an emotional release. Uriel warmly welcomes us into the arms of his love and helps us let go emotional baggage that keeps us from moving forward. Uriel is able to help with depression, anxiety fear, fear, and anger.

Signs the Archangel Uriel may be communicating and present in your life

* Sparks in electricity. Did you notice that lately there are more light bulb failures? That the flame on your gas burner is jumping higher than normal? You might be experiencing static electricity, or little electrical shocks throughout the day. These are all signs Uriel exists, and can help you to transform sparks into flames so you can fulfill your destiny.

* You feel called. By reaching out to others, we help ourselves. This is the beauty and complexity of life. Any action, no matter how small or large, is taken seriously and has a consequence. Uriel might be supporting you

and encouraging you to reach for others. On the road to helping others, you might find the answers that you are searching for, the motivation you lack or the thing that makes all this make sense.

* Lightbulb moments. These are what I like to call A-Ha Moments. The moment you find yourself stuck and hopeless after a long period of struggle, when suddenly a solution springs to your mind. Uriel deserves to be thanked for this momentous inspiration.

* Red is most closely associated to Uriel. This is because it's the color of energy and fire. Red also has an associated stop-and go energy. It is symbolic of energy and can also serve to warn that you should not proceed unless you have more information. Uriel is your friend, giving wisdom, clarity, and the time is now for movement.

Connecting to Uriel

Uriel is the archangel associated with movement, transformation, change. It is only natural that rituals to invoke him include these elements.

Uriel's presence and guidance is what I seek through music, movement and song.

For the element fire, energy, and transformation to be added, start by lighting candles. As the candles are lit, you can recite any purifying blessings. This could be a favorite script, or you can simply say "I call The Protectors of the Four Directions and ask They cleanse and protect the sacred space." I do so with an open, receptive, and grateful heart.

Next, decide on your music. You might be wondering why I didn't put music selection as the first step. I have found myself in situations where I had my music picked out for an Invocation Ritual, only to find that the music did not suit the mood and energy. Sometimes you don't know what music will work best until it is already working. If you prefer to work within the sacred circle of protection and don't want to get out, you might bring some music with you. I am aware of many people who object to technology in these types if rituals. I have no problems using a smartphone or tablet. The vast array of music available gives me an unlimited selection. If you feel the device interferes with energy, do not go for it. However, if your energy is stable, your tablet and phone can still be helpful.

From there, you just need to move. Sway, dance, wiggle. Do whatever is most comfortable for you. My favourite rituals include music and movement. I love the feeling of a rhythm that moves from slow speed to fast again.

Uriel encourages you to call out and reflect on the transformative nature your movement. You are constantly moving through the time, changing your body. You can't return to the place you were when the music started. Uriel can help you to focus your intention when you ask. What are you seeking guidance with?

You don't know where you are. What are your goals?

Uriel was a great help. Although you may feel immediately transformed by Uriel's guidance, it is possible that your energy will grow over time. Uriel is always available for messages via all channels of communication. The service of the Archangels is consistent, but they can be flexible with communication.

Haniel - The Angel of Love Joy and Endless Blessings

Haniel can be described as an archangel of Joy, similar to Gabriel. Haniel's message about joy and blessings differs from Gabriel's because she is more focused than Gabriel on the areas where joy will grow and blossom. Haniel energy is available in areas such as home, family and relationships. Haniel can be perceived as a woman and embodies feminine power.

Haniel's guidance is meant to assist us in our search of spiritual fulfillment. She knows that even though our spirit is pure essence and our bodies are made of the physical universe, we still need to find fulfillment and joy in this world to attain the spiritual fulfillment that she seeks.

Haniel helps you to overcome obstacles that keep you from experiencing the joys and blessings of life. She believes that everyone is blessed, regardless where they are on their journey. Through her influence, we can see silver linings through the clouds and the rainbow.

Signs the Archangel Haniel Is Present and Communicating in Your Life

* I love to be able to feel Haniel in my life, even when it seems dark. Yes, it is easy to tell someone this when they are going through something traumatic or difficult. This is an entirely different matter. It is that moment when all you see is hope and beauty. Haniel brings peace and joy into your heart.

Haniel is there to help you when you stumble across a new passion or joy. Sometimes, we get stuck in a rut. We don't realize the joys and possibilities that await us. Haniel is there to help us find our soul's happiness, which often comes from the most unexpected of places.

* You feel inexplicably lightened. Are you familiar with situations where stress and difficulty can physically weigh you down? You work hard every day until finally you are free. You will feel lighter spiritually as well as physically without any noticeable changes to your circumstances. Haniel is here to support you as you carry the weight. She does all this because she knows you are in need of relief.

* Haniel is strongly associated with the color turquoise. It is a sign that she cares deeply about you and guides you joyfully.

Haniel Connecting

Haniel connects with you gently and intuitively. Just be open to receiving her guidance, filling your heart with love, and then embracing her as she is.

Haniel likes to be invoked by me with a ritual of prayer/blessing that includes light, soft colors and textures.

Begin by creating an altar to your invitation. Consider lighting a small candle, white, pink or turquoise. Add small items that bring you joy, or that symbolize love. Haniel is sure to be drawn to these items.

Why should we set up an altar? Haniel isn't interested in taking these things. They bring her joy and love. In addition to that, she recognizes that if one has taken the time and surrounded herself with trinkets of joy and loving energy, it is already a significant amount of the work.

As you sit at an altar, call Haniel with your request. You must focus on your purpose. Visualize your purpose as a bubble. Fill it with love, joyous energy. Haniel is the one who will receive your bubble.

You should close your altar with the same intention as when you first set it up. When you are done, bless the altar with a quick blessing of security and love. Take any flowers you used on the altar and place them outside under the moonlight in gratitude to Haniel. You don't need to use any flowers. Place a small token of love and joy underneath the moon for just one night. You will be rewarded with many blessings.

Raziel: Archangel, Mysteries, and Revelations

There are many secrets within the universe. Raziel has every one of them.

Raziel is a presence in the life of someone who has reached the point where they are open to new truths. This usually happens during a time of spiritual growth or search. Raziel is the guardian of divine mysteries and the one who knows all the answers.

Raziel will give you a deeper, more powerful sense of intuition. Raziel is often the one that someone calls upon when they are trying to develop their psychic and intuitive abilities. He can get rid of the clutter and remove any cobwebs between us, the spiritual world, and him.

Signs the Archangel Raziel Is Present and Communicating with You

* You start seeing rainbows. Raziel is so connected to all the mysteries and hidden secrets of the universe that he associates with each color. Raziel can bring out more rainbows.

* Your intuition suddenly feels strong and on target. I believe in listening to my intuition. You may not always be able to recognize how right your intuition was. It is necessary to wait for life's events to unfold before everything makes sense. Raziel is on your side so you don't have to wait for life's events. You'll feel more confident and focused in your intuition, and it will confirm almost immediately that you are right.

* You feel closer to the divine. Raziel is a spiritual guide and mentor for those who seek guidance and development. Raziel can help you get through the stages of doubt and ask questions along the way. Raziel can help you feel more connected with your spirituality and a stronger connection to the mysteries.

* You have an abundance of creative inspiration. Raziel knows that creative activity sparks and encourages inner discovery. If you do something creative you open yourself to a completely new wavelength, which makes

you more open and receptive for subtle energies from the universe.

Raziel Connecting

Raziel, from my experience isn't always the easiest to find. It's not because Raziel doesn't want to hear the idea. It is more that you have to do more to open yourself up to his energy.

You must be open to the mysteries, and the secrets, of the divine realm. Truth be told, many of us say we want to, but are closed and inaccessible. You can communicate with Raziel by praying or meditation on how to be more open to his energies.

You can also bring any type or activity that is spiritual or divinatory to his attention. Raziel is happy to help you. The source of your intentions is important. The goal might be to increase your spiritual connection, improve your intuition, create more, or develop psychic skills. But what are you really preventing yourself from achieving your goals? You have the potential and the will to achieve your goals. The ability is already within you. So what are you waiting for? Raziel is able to clear blockages and other obstacles that can hinder the flow or energy. Do not be surprised if it is emotionally exhausting.

By Your Side, Day & Night

The archangels can be a constant presence in any situation. They are always available to help you, no matter what time it is. They guide and protect you often without you knowing it. I am frequently asked "Why do I need them to help me?".

They will always be there to guide and protect you, even if you don't acknowledge it. However, if you have special requests or require additional assistance, or feel a greater sense of connection, let them be aware that you're at a stage in your life where you are open to their energies. This is your life. You must be the one to open up communication channels and request what you want. You never know until you ask. Even if the answer is not what you expected, there is no request that an archangel cannot fulfill.

Connecting With Angels: Inviting the Angels, Communicating and Recognizing Your Energies

Chapter 3 Spiritual Support Team meeting

Angels are there for you no matter where and what you do. They are with you every step of the way, protecting and guiding you. My first experience with the angels being there for me was not pleasant. There aren't many people who live a perfect existence, and I didn't like the idea that they could see the angelic side to me. And guess what? They don't care.

To meet your angels, also called your Spiritual Support Team or SST, the first step is to learn how to get over yourself. Angels live in an entirely different realm to us. They see us entirely differently from what we see. In the mirror you might see an imperfect, flawed being. They see the complete opposite.

Your angels perceive you as the pure, radiant energy and light of all the universe. Your angels have not seen you live a human life. They view all of our thoughts as part and parcel of the overall process. They aren't there to judge you in your times of weakness, anger, or despair. It is their job help you to get past your most embarrassing moments and to guide you along the right path. This is an extremely difficult life. There are many failures, pitfalls, and trials. This is all part of the point. We're here to learn and grow from this experience. We can't do it without some embarrassing moments, or years. It is possible to disconnect from your SST if you believe that the angelic realm has all the answers. Be open to their presence and forget your ego.

In the introduction to the book, I talked about the different angelic/spiritual energies that guide and monitor us. Some people believe there is one angel, one spirit guide or one angel that watches over you. I believe we have many. I call them Spiritual Support Team (SST).

Your SST can be described as your heavenly support team. As humans it is easier to understand angels and spirit guide when we imagine them as human and put them in situations which are relevant to our everyday lives. You will be able to bear with me while I try to do that here.

Your life is a journey as the CEO of your company. A great support team is vital to any CEO's success. There will be multiple levels of support staff, each with its own strengths and weaknesses. This is your SST.

Your archangels are the most powerful. They can and will assist you in any situation. They will be there to give advice and help you navigate your way.

The next step is to have a personal secretary. This is your SST angel. This angel is with you always, from the moment your soul was created until the moment you leave the physical realm. Your guardian is your guide and protector in all aspects of your day-today life. It is their voice you hear whispering into your ear each day. Once you can attune to angelic energy you will start to see the signs in your life and appreciate how strong their presence is.

Finally, the worker-bees of your business. These are your angels. These are those you call on when you need help with a particular task. Although angels and archangels both play an important role within your life, archangels tend to be more present in difficult or unusual times. You can call Angels at any hour of the day or night to get help with your problems. Angels can also be contacted if you have an "errand" to run. For example, you can pray to an angel and ask them to be with your loved ones or to help you through a difficult time in your life.

There might be occasions when you have an additional to your SST. This could be a little bit like a special consultant. Your spirit guides are the ones I am referring too. These beings are not technically angels. An angel by definition has never walked on earth in human form. Spirit guides have. Spirit guides are sometimes called ghosts. This is because they may be the spirit energy that has passed on from our lives to the spirit realm. The negative connotations that ghost can have on some are hauntings, dark energy, and other things make me hesitate to use this term. You should know that your spirit guides are not dark energy. They come to you with no ill-will, regardless of any past relationships. Spirit guides are not angels and cannot change the course of a journey. For example your guardian Angel may cause you or someone else to alter your route, or intervene in any other way to prevent an accident. However, a spirit guide doesn't have that power. Although they can sometimes give guidance if they know of a situation that could be problematic, this is not the extent of their power. They are here to give you guidance, comfort, and sometimes answer your questions.

The one thing you shouldn't allow to enter your business is a member from the spiritual realm. It is called a negative or dark-energy force. Even though this type is present in the spiritual realms, we rarely have to interact with them. Instead, our SST takes them out before they even get a chance. Most negative energy is made up of beings who once walked on the earth. But, because of one reason or another, they are stuck there. They have never learned how to let go, or been trained as a spirit guide. These are the ones that make you feel anxious or afraid. They should be avoided. If you do come into contact, you should immediately leave the room and call upon the archangel Michael to extinguish the influence and protect your health.

Now that you've been introduced to the members of your support group, it is time for you and them to get to know each other. Every member of your team should have a personal relationship with a great CEO. Let's discuss rituals and ceremonies to invoke angelic power.

Rituals & Ceremonies to Invoke Angelic Energy

There are numerous books written on it. However, you don't need much to call your angels. This is because it is already here. It already surrounds and exists. If this is true, then it's worth the effort. Here are the reasons rituals, ceremonies, and other rituals are essential to your relationship with angels.

Your vibrational energy will increase, which will enable your angels become more powerful and you to be more aware that they are there.

This is your life, and it's up to you to participate. You are just letting others do all your work. This is not a fulfilling experience and does not allow you to grow spiritually.

Sometimes the angelic energy around us needs to be focused. Angels can be busy. You can think about the archangels. The seven mentioned above do more than serve you. Even the most multitaskers need to stay on top of what's happening. By calling your angels, you can help them put their energy where it's needed.

Gratitude and gratitude are important. There is always give and take. There are always a reaction to any action. Or at least that's what should happen. We do our part to balance the energy in the universe when we show gratitude. Angels appreciate gratitude just as much and deserve our respect.

Rituals are a way to feel more connected. This is our human nature.

Prayer to the Four Directions Archangels

This is an invocation that I enjoy using often. It can be used every day, once per week, or as often as you feel is necessary.

To invoke the Archangels Raphael Gabriel, Gabriel, and Michael in this ritual, focus your energy, intent, and intention into each of the directions. All archangels possess power; however, the specific angels who created the four directional energy pillars are the most powerful. They can be a constant and strong force in your daily life.

Before I pray, my sacred circle is prepared. This doesn't have be a difficult process. You can purify the space physically by clearing it out (removing clutter, cleaning up the floor, sweeping it up, etc.) and then lighting a candle to heat the air.

If you desire, you may increase your energy by adding personal artifacts and items like stones.

Before you begin, take some time to calm your mind and center. Take deep, long breaths. Feel the white light protecting you.

Begin by looking to the east, your arms open, and invoke ArchangelUriel.

To invoke Uriel, say "With purity and spirit I invoke Uriel to enter the space in front. I ask you to bless me with all the clarity, grace, and wisdom that I need in order to be of your service. I ask for your guidance on how I can be of greatest service to you, me and humanity. (Insert a specific query or request if necessary. Your presence is appreciated today and every day.

Next, face the south while keeping your arms open. This will invoke Archangel Raphael.

Say, "With purity and spirit, i invoke Raphael. Please bless my ability to let things go that are no longer necessary and give me the courage to accept the blessings into my life. I ask that you lighten the path to total and complete healing. (Insert specific query or request, if appropriate. Your presence is appreciated today and every day.

Next, turn towards the west, keeping your arms wide open, invoking Archangel Gabriel.

To invoke Gabriel, say "With purity and spirit, Please grant me the spiritual strength and fortitude to face my fears and overcome them so that my life can fulfill its purpose. (Insert a specific question, if possible.) Your presence is appreciated today and every day.

Now, turn your face north, keeping your arms open, to invoke Archangel Michael.

Simply say, "With purityof heart and spirit I invoke Michael into the space to your left. Please grant me wisdom, love, and the ability to communicate with you. Let me hear truth, see and speak truth from a loving heart. Your love and wisdom will lead me down the path of wisdom. If possible, ask a specific question. Your presence is appreciated today and every day.

Now picture the four archangels creating love and healing energy in a protective environment. Close your eyes. Feel the energy moving around you like an unborn infant, in the safe, warm and protective environment of your mother's womb.

This is a time to take a deep breath and allow the energy around you and above you to relax. Feel the protection. Let go of all worries, fear, or negativity. There is no place here for it, in the arms of your Angels.

Visualize the energy sealing around yourself, so there are no opportunities for negative emotions and influences.

Express gratitude to all four archangels again. Use the words that make you most at ease right now.

At this point you should feel the energy fade slightly as the archangels leave you. This will allow you to move freely out of the circle.

Be aware of the energies of Archangels throughout the day and pay close attention to signs they use for communication.

Ritual for FaceTime with Your Guardian Angel

We all have a guardian angel. That includes you.

It is possible to feel as though your guardian angel has lost touch with you. It doesn't matter how lonely you feel, an angel is always there to help you.

Is it possible to have bad things happen even though you have a guardian-angel? Too many people associate the image of guardian-angels with the ideal of a perfect life that is free from suffering, injury, and tragedy. I want you to know that before you were given this body, you made a promise to live a human, full life with all its blessings. This is a journey. To truly experience this experience and grow spiritually, you need to accept the bad with the positive, the bittersweet with the sweet.

It may not be clear yet but you know what your end goal is. There are some things that you have to do, people that must be met, experiences that must be had. You will fall along the way. This is a reality. If you do not intend to take clear danger into consideration, your guardian will help you get up. It is impossible to expect your guardian Angel to alter your destiny.

Have you ever wondered what it would be like to meet your guardian? I like to meet with my guardian angel once in a while. You can do it! Absolutely. Do you think they would enjoy a cup of coffee with you? Caffeine makes it jittery for me and can interfere with my energy field. So I haven't tried. Instead, I have created my own ritual for quietly communicating with my guardian Angel in my house that I would love to share with all of you.

Planning what I want is the first step to setting up a chat appointment with my guardian Angel. Although it's possible to skip this step and just go with the flow, I think it adds structure and focus. I have tried this ritual before without any predetermined thoughts or questions. But, while I made contact with my guardian angel, it felt like something was missing. My one-on-1 time is what makes me feel complete and productive. I don't want to waste energy or lose focus wondering what I should say.

While you can do this quickly, it is better to do it earlier than later. My thoughts and questions are organized the day before I plan the ritual. I keep a journal specifically dedicated to my guardian angel where I write down all of my thoughts, feelings and queries. This journal is usually found near my bed. It allows me to write down any dreams that may come up. You can use your journal or any other tool. You can either write it out or save it to your phone.

Before you begin the ritual. What patterns do you notice in your thoughts? Sometimes patterns tell us more than just the questions.

Once you feel grounded within your intention, it's time to begin the ritual.

It is important to sit in a comfortable and relaxed position. Place yourself in a position that is comfortable enough for you not to feel the need of reaching for your hands or trying to adjust. Be aware that too much comfort can lead to you becoming too comfortable. You might feel too relaxed to make contact with your angels. There is a happy balance. You just need to find the right spot. There is no right or incorrect position.

Breathe deeply and relax your eyes. You can imagine the air you breathe being pure and filled by the divine spirit. Continue this process until you can no longer focus on the imagery in your breath. You should eventually find it comes easily.

After your breathing is steady and filling you up with divine lights, visualize a light over you. The color of the light you choose is up to your imagination, but don't be too focused. Let the light choose the first color that comes into your mind. Your guardian angel can see the color you see. If the light you see isn't what you want, don't worry.

For a few reasons, a dark or negative feeling light might appear. First, you may be feeling anxious about the ritual. If you feel apprehensive or anxious about the ritual, then stop and start breathing in the protective divine lights. Keep doing this until your body is relaxed and comfortable.

You may also see a darker and more intense color because that is the color that is associated with your guardian. Black, for example is a color that draws in energy. This color is often linked to "soul sucking" or other negative entities. You can think of it in another way. The transformation of energy occurs when it is put into something. Black is transformative. Black attracts any white light. A black energy energy field is full of white, positive energy that is very protective. What are you experiencing in your daily life that your guardian angel is bringing to you with this highly protective, transformative energy. If the answer to that question is clear, then you don't have to be worried. Your guardian angel just represents the energy it needs for protection in your current state.

Sometimes, however, you might accidentally call upon a less-than-friendly spirit. If you have attempted to center yourself with divine light before and still feel relaxed, comfortable and calm, but then suddenly this light appears and causes you to feel uneasy, simply stop. If you are unable to invite any spirits or energy, say so and tell them that they will not be allowed in. To purify spiritual air, you don't need much more than that. Don't be too concerned about it. This energy won't make you feel ill and can do no harm. Do not let it get you down.

Now, it's time to go back to our ritual. You can now imagine the light surrounding you. This light will increase the energy and vibration around.

This light will be directed at your heart chakra, so imagine it shining down upon you. Feel the energy pulse with every heartbeat. You are connecting with your guardian angel's energy and your life force. You might feel your pulse beat strong throughout your body or your body start to tingle. This is your vibrational level rising. You can feel this sensation by sitting down.

Do it when you feel confident. You can either copy the one already provided or create one. You are your guardian angel, and you know him better than anyone.

"I invoke their presence, my guardian angels who protect and serve me with their love and gentle guidance. I ask that they come to me now, when my own energy and vibrations have been rising, so that our connection can be both visual and spirit. Thank you so much for your love, support, and guidance. Come into this sacred place and be yourself now. "Thank you!"

Keep your eyes shut and wait for the image from your guardian Angel to show up. Don't force it. It is easy to think that your guardian angel will appear in one direction, but they could be completely different. Let the image grow and change at its pace.

If you do not see a distinct picture, don't worry. Your guardian angel can visit you via any of your senses. You might feel a light touch on your arm or notice a pleasant, unexpected smell. Keep an open mind and pay attention to all your senses.

Once you feel confident that you have reached out to your guardian angel you may bring your questions and concerns. Your guardian angel is not in the same place as you. They have never been on an earthly plane. They are not capable of communicating in the same manner as us. Instead, you can listen with your brain for the answers. These could come in the form clairvoyance and clairaudience or your inner voice.

Now, sit still and focus on the breath. You will get your answers. Be open and open to all possible answers. Pay attention and pay attention to sensory sensations around. Anything you observe at this moment is your angel communicating directly with you.

If you feel comfortable, it's possible to continue the conversation in an easier manner until you feel ready to close the session. You'll know when it is.

Release your tension, increase your vibration and call in the divine energy. You can also release your guardian angel by thanking them for their love and continued service.

Invoking your guardian angel is a sure way to get answers. They are there in order to protect, guide, and love. They want to talk to you. All that is required to make the connection is your willingness to listen.

Prayer to your Angels in Urgent and Immediate Needs

Each one of us in this world will experience a moment in which we need protection immediately. Although these are unlikely to happen often, it does happen. In these situations, it is important to not waste your time and energy on a lengthy, tedious ritual. You should instead make your need clear and urgent.

Your angels always stand by you and are ready and available to assist you. You can use this quick prayer in order to reach your angels when you're in immediate need.

Angels of Heaven

God sent you here to protect and care for me. I ask that at this very moment you take me under your protective light and cover me with your wings.

I ask that you give me wisdom, strength, and protection for those times when I am unable.

This will help to lift your feelings of fear, anxiety, desolation, anger, and other emotions. Please replace them with your ever-loving and protective light.

I appeal to you to help in my present struggle.

Amen

Create the Path Ritual for Your Angels

Have you ever felt completely lost in a foreign land? This is not about being lost in another place, or when your GPS doesn't work. No, I am not referring to the times that life puts a blindfold across your eyes, twists you around, and leaves you struggling to find your feet and orient yourself.

These difficult times are hard on the soul.

This is a time to call in your angels. Ask them to help you clear the path so you may travel along it.

Although I enjoy performing this ritual outdoors it is possible to perform it at home. Nature is generally free from obstructions, which is why I love to be outdoors. There are no walls behind me, no furniture to be messed with. These are only symbolic. This ritual should be done in an open area. If this is the case, you need to make sure that your angels have a clear vision of what it looks like.

There are a few things I like to add to the angelic ritual. These items can be left out. Your ritual should be reflective of you and your relationship to your angels. However, I feel these props add an extra energy to the ceremony--and they are also fun.

Here is a quick list with some of my favorite things:

* A knife can be used to carve the path or push the obstacles out of the way. (I've used everything from a beautifully decorated carving knife and a kid's plastic craft-dough sculpting "knife".

* A sheer, transparent piece of cloth used to symbolize both the veil between my physical and spiritual planes and also the veil that is being lifted out of my line of vision.

* Symbolism to my struggles (a heart-shaped boulder for relationship issues; an empty notebook for academic struggles; a pomegranate in fertility; etc.

* Incense or a flame to represent fire to burn away obstructions

* A feather used to indicate angelic involvement

Once you have your items organized, you will need to find a place to sit down or stand. You will be using visualizations to help you pray, so ensure that you are comfortable.

Relax and take a deep breath to calm down.

Think about your current struggle. Do you feel blocked in any area? Are you sure where the blockage is coming from? What do think is the main issue?

Do you believe there is an archangel who can help you? Your angels have the ability to help you. If your sight or path is getting blocked due to significant energy, an archangel can be called in. If you do, you will call the Archangel to seek help. But, you must decide beforehand if it is something you want.

Now visualize the protective heavenly glow coming down and flowing through you. Allow all negativity to go and let your energy increase.

You can say the following prayer with your energy flowing through.

Angels Of God, designated by Our Heavenly Mother to be ever present at My Side, I Thank You for Your enduring, endless service.

(If needed, invoke the archangel.

I ask that your arms lift me into your embrace, and that you help me see beyond what is happening in my world. I ask that you lead me in the direction that will allow me fulfil my soul's purpose.

I have been carrying a lot of weight on my shoulders and am now tired and weak. I need your help to navigate the path that lies ahead of me.

For your unyielding support and love, what can I do to show you my appreciation? Show me the way. Let me know how I can help you.

Please send to heaven my prayers for clarity, guidance, and protection.

Amen.

After you have said the prayer, take a moment to relax and allow the protective heavenly light to continue flowing through you.

Slowly allow the light to pass in front of your eyes and let it part so you may see beyond.

Which is the first thing you notice? Don't overthink it. It doesn't matter if it's not clear to you right now.

Let the scene grow until you feel satisfied. You shouldn't rush but don't be discouraged from waiting for the next step. Your angels are showing your a clear image of the path. This is the path that will guide you in the right direction. This path is not always the one that we want.

In your prayer, ask God if there is a way you can give thanks. For clues, look for clues. The angels might not ask for anything, but it is possible they are asking for a favor. All requests should be honored.

Don't be afraid of asking for clarification if needed. Sometimes communication will not be easy. Ask your angels to help you better understand or provide you with more subtle meanings or imagery. It is okay to ask. Wait for them to answer. If they don't, pay close attention to your surroundings the rest of the morning and to the imagery in the night.

Your angels can communicate with you by finding a way.

An Angel's Wisdom: A Short Ritual For Enlightenment

The spirit realm contains all the knowledge necessary to understand the universe. The answers to every question can be found in the hands and feet of the heavenly beings.

If the answers exist, why is it so difficult for us to find them.

It's both complicated and easy to answer this question. When your soul committed to living an earthly, it also made an agreement to forget the answers. This is because to truly grow spiritually, your soul must experience the trials of searching for those answers. Gabriel, who is the archangel that protects and blesses the unborn child before birth, erases any universal knowledge from an infant's brain. Each of our journeys begins with a clean slate. We have the opportunity to learn along the way.

It doesn't necessarily mean that we shouldn't ask for help and guidance when searching for the answers. When faced with a difficult situation at work or a research project, would you simply wander aimlessly in search of the answers? Or would you look for them immediately from the places you already knew they existed? We make it harder for ourselves to ask our angels for some wisdom, rather than making things easier.

I love to invoke Uriel and Jophiel for this brief wisdom ritual. Jophiel is the angel of wisdom, understanding, judgement. You can invoke any one or all of them depending on what you're comfortable with.

Start by finding somewhere quiet and comfortable to sit down. Let go of all distractions and just relax.

Once you feel relaxed and calm, you can start to focus on the issue or the situation in which you seek wisdom. Focus on your thoughts and be very clear.

Picture a yellowish orange light shining in front. The archangels can be seen emerging from the light.

They are warm and open their arms to welcome you into their world, and they radiate the warmth from the light towards your soul, brightening your mind and the energy space around you.

Spread your arms out and reach your sides. Feel the golden light drift around your fingers.

Your hands should be raised above your head. You can place one thumb on each temple. Finally, you can place your remaining fingers across your forehead.

Gently move your fingers towards your eyes. Make sure your index fingers are still connected above the third eye of your forehead. This creates a link between your intuitive vision and your physical eyes.

These three sentences should be repeated three times:

Your divine wisdom flows into and guides me from Heavenly Angels.

Heavenly angels, guide my steps and grant me the wisdom I need right now.

Heavenly angels! Thank you for your wisdom and understanding.

Now release the archangels. Do you feel differently about this situation? Do you have new insight? Are you feeling more optimistic?

If you do not have immediate answers, then pay close attention to any messages your angels might send you during the next three working days.

Peace in Your Heart, Peace within Your Mind

The world around us is filled with chaos energy.

As a sentient entity, you are bound absorb some of this energy. Add to it the fact you likely have other things that cause stress and anxiety in your life, and you can create an uneasy mind and a hurting heart.

These are the moments when you'll need something to help you feel whole, calm, and peaceful again.

This simple ritual will get you there.

When I started to use this method, I had it written down on a piece and kept it in my bag. It was convenient to always have it with me, as I always felt immediate relief.

You can use this ritual to help you feel more peaceful and relaxed the next time that you feel uneasy or anxious.

Make sure you find somewhere quiet and with as few distractions, as possible. This ritual is best done at home. It is possible to perform this ritual in your car or at work, as I have personally experienced it.

Begin by spending some time inhaling and exhaling slowly.

Imagine the sky filled with beautiful purple and golden clouds as you breathe.

Unveiled from the clouds is an angel in the most beautiful purple robes. His wings and face are covered in gold.

Hold your index finger in your hand and place it on his forehead. Repeat this three times.

Imagine his gentle light entering your brain. You instantly feel calm, relaxed and at home.

Ask yourself what you think.

"The divine light and peace that flows through me. I am centered. "I am at peace, with my angel's light beside.

Continue repeating this mantra till you feel calmed, centered, and peaceful.

Be grateful to the angels who brought you peace and energy. Then, let them go and open your eyes.

Chapter 4 Affirmation Ritual for Forgiveness

Forgiveness is one the most difficult internal processes. It doesn't matter if you are the one asking for it. Sometimes it takes some emotional work to reach the point of forgiveness.

It is helpful to call in your angels at times like this. This ritual is one I enjoy because it centers on love and gratitude. It helps us accept others as they are, human and imperfect.

This ritual can also modified to ask angelic guidance for those who are in need.

If you'd like, you can call in your own angels or an archangel. Although not often mentioned, Zadkiel is the archangel of forgiveness, mercy and tolerance. If you need a stronger angelic presence in your life, he can be called upon for this ritual.

You will need to light one candle. It is best to light a single candle in white or violet to boost the energy and enhance the magic of the ritual.

After lighting the candle, you can now close your eyes. Imagine a lavender light surrounding yourself.

If you know of an angel that you would like to work alongside, this is the time to reach out to them and ask their help.

Think of the person you are angry with. Do not try to ignore your feelings. You can't heal or forgive yourself if your angels aren't fully present and open with you.

Imagine the light of the candle rising toward the heavens. As the candle grows, so does its healing, transformative power.

Imagine yourself still wrapped in the protective lavender light as you walk towards the flame. Fear not, the flame can burn you. This is a purifying light that will cleanse you and help you release any pain.

As you walk into the flame, say

I forgive (enter a name) from the bottom of my heart.

I remove hurt and pain from my life and replace it with healing, loving love.

I am free from all anger toward (enter name).

I am cleansed and made to spread the light.

Before you abandon the flame, ask your angels if they can guide you and protect you. This will enable you to feel forgiveness and love when you are struggling.

Now, calmly walk away from the flame. With love in your heart, you can leave anger and hurt behind and bring healing and love energy to its place.

You can write down your affirmations and use them throughout the day if you feel anger or hurt.

You can thank your angels for their support and ask them to send you forgiving energy towards the person that caused you distress.

It is sometimes us that need to forgive for our actions towards others or ourselves. To forgive yourself for being angry or disappointed, you can use the affirmation ritual.

Angelic Meditation: Spread Love Energy

I can't recall a moment when we didn't need a little more love.

This meditation is simply beautiful because it allows us to share our gentle, loving energy. I do use it to focus my attention on people or situations that are near me.

This meditation is beautiful when you are experiencing the chaos energy of the universe and wish to bring healing through unconditional love. It's a great choice when you are surrounded by people who need healing and love. Sometimes words are just not enough. In these cases, it's time to call on the angels for help.

This meditation is easy. It doesn't require any special props. And it only takes a few seconds. It's a wonderful addition to any routine of meditation.

You will need to find somewhere quiet and relaxing where you can rest comfortably.

Take a few deep, cleansing inhalations.

Breathe in the rhythm of it and allow it to relax you.

Gather any negative thoughts and feelings, then wrap them in bubbles.

Bring the bubble you hold in your hands upwards towards the sky and exhale.

Follow it, as it floats up, further and farther away from yourself, until finally it bursts.

As the fragments fall, visualize them changing into positive, loving energy as they fly through the sky.

Let go of any negativity. Now focus on bringing in the loving light of Heaven into your body. Let the light of heaven flow through you and over you, completely covering you in loving energy.

While you are wrapped in the blanket, visualize your angel in front. Take the image that you see. Do not try and influence the angel's appearance. Just let it happen.

The angel that appears in your life, you can tell:

"Guardian angel watching over me, please take my love and share it (or for a general purpose use, say "share this with those on the earth")

Assist them in their daily lives, be there to guide and love them until their soul is free from all limitations.

They can dry their tears and let go of all their pain.

We are all connected and share the love-filled power of the heavens.

Amen."

Imagine the blanket surrounding you reaching out into all the world. Your angel can receive it and wrap it around the recipients.

Next, close the meditation by thanking your angels. Refocus on your breath until you feel compelled.

Allow the peaceful energy of meditation to accompany you throughout your day.

Simple Prayer for Gratitude

There is always something to be grateful every day. Even in our darkest times, there is still a way to express gratitude. I believe that these are the times when your spirit develops and grows.

Sometimes the most ordinary things can be reasons for gratitude. Do you think that anything extraordinary has occurred to inspire feelings of gratitude The day's inevitability is sufficient to inspire gratitude.

Your angels will always be by your side. Their service is selfless, and it never ends. They may not always want our gratitude, however they are always deserving it.

This prayer does not ask for anything of your angels. It does not include a request for guidance or wisdom. This is not an expectation.

This prayer is something that I try to do every morning. I love to feel valued and appreciated when I begin my day. You have the option to choose when and how often your angels are thanked for their presence in you life.

"Heavenly father, I thank you for opening the heavens and blessings me with the angels whom you have chosen to guide me.

Recognize my gratitude for their ever-lasting service.

And to you my angelic guides who watch me with a tender heart and protective eyes, my love, gratitude, and service is yours.

Amen."

20 Signs Angels Communicate With Us Everyday: Recognizing the Signs of Communication

Angels are everywhere we look every day.

They are there every moment of our lives. Why is it so difficult for most of us to recognise their presence? Why do we need to have a "feeling" they are there? Why can't we communicate with them in concrete ways?

Communication with your angels can be very different from chatting with your best friend. We do not physically see or hear them.

Instead, we rely upon the subtle energy transfer across the barrier that separates the spiritual and the earthly planes. Instead of hearing the voice with our ears and listening for it with our hearts, we should listen for the voice we feel with our heart.

Angels recognize the difficulties of this kind of communication. It can be difficult and often leave us asking ourselves if angels are even real.

Perhaps that is why angels have come up with ways to communicate directly with you using the same means they use to see, hear, and feel. There are many symbols that can be associated with angelic presence.

How did these symbols come to be associated with angelic communications? It is not possible to translate the words from heaven. Therefore, we must interpret these symbols as best we can. Numerous times these symbols have been used to indicate angelic presence. Many people have shared stories about their angels and these symbol, with common threads. We who are the most attuned have discovered that these symbols are clearly signs of communication.

I do not expect you will accept all this until you have personally experienced it. This is because you will be more open and able to communicate with your angels. When you recognize the symbolic ways in which they communicate, you will see more of them in daily life. This will allow you to connect your everyday experiences with your angels immediately, and it will all make sense.

Keep a journal to help you connect with your angels. It will be useful to note all occasions you have encountered the following angelic communication methods. Keep track of the exact time, place and circumstances. You might be feeling spiritually lost. Then suddenly, a sign of communication arrived. Was it a sign you saw right before something bad happened? Is it an ordinary day but something clicked the next morning and it made sense that your Angel was speaking to me? Don't force your angels to speak to you. Let it happen. I promise it will all be obvious.

Below are some signs of angelic communication that I have found most commonly. This isn't a comprehensive list. Your angels are as familiar with you as you are yourself. They will communicate to you and get attention in ways they are confident you will respond to. Your angel may be communicating with you even though you can't see it. Keep an open mind to the subtler ways that angels communicate with you.

Feathers

This is one of my favourite signs that an angel has spoken to me. We associate angels having large, feathery and graceful wings. It makes sense that one can sometimes fall. It is possible that one of your angels may be greeting you by dropping a feather.

A feather found in a place you would not expect to find one is more likely a sign of your angels. You may find feathers on the ground when you pass large flocks of geese or if you are walking around a lake. Could these be signs from angels? Absolutely. Could it be possible that the geese are losing some feathers as well? This answer is also correct. Use your intuition. You may believe your angels have spoken to you.

You can almost always find a random feather when you go on a walk. It's usually a sign that your angels are greeting you. White is associated with heaven and angels. However, angels also have many other colors. It is important to be aware of unusual feathers, such as red, purple, or blue. This could mean that one the archangels might be communicating with or guiding you.

Butterflies

Butterflies are lovely creatures. They are delicate and light but can travel amazing distances through difficult conditions. When I see a butterfly, especially one that is not in a group, I think about my angels. The single butterfly is almost certain to be an angel saying hello.

What is your angel trying tell you? Think of the life span of a butterfly. It is transformative. It undergoes great changes and periods of isolation before blossoming into its full beauty. It has a happy, social, fluttering, and joyful energy. It almost seems playful as it flies and floats in the breeze. Children love to chase butterfly's, which could be because children still have the ability see and feel the angelic energy they carry.

Pennies

How can you get Pennies from the Heavens? It could actually be true.

It has been long associated with good luck finding a random coin, but some believe that it is your angel bestowing the blessing. A random penny can give us a moment of joy. It is a gift.

There are three things that you can do when you have a find penny. The first is to ignore the penny, which I don't recommend. Accepting any sign of communication is the best way to build a stronger connection with your angels. The second option is to keep it and keep it as an angel of luck or love. You can use it as a good luck charm to remind yourself that you aren't alone.

You can either give it to someone else or you can keep it. I try to pass every penny I find onto someone, even if I don't feel like holding on to it. This could be for a child, someone in line at the shop who is a few pennies short on their payment or for a charity money drop box. I might send a thank you note to the angels. Then, I will leave the penny there where I know someone will be able to find it. Give blessings and they'll come back to your.

Rainbows

There is science behind rainbows. There is a physical reason why they exist. This is what I use to argue that rainbows come from the angels. While it is true that rainbows appear for a reason (though they can be beautiful and have a lot of power), you might not believe that this is the case.

The presence of rainbows without obvious rainbow-causing conditions is a sure sign that your angel is reaching for you. An angelic presence can be seen by looking up at the skies and seeing small rainbow reflections or raindrops. You might also see unusually abundant rainbow patterns all at once.

Clouds

Angels come from heaven. It makes sense therefore that when we look upward, we may see a sign of them.

Remember the game you played with your angels as a kid, in which you looked into the skies and tried to find images among the clouds. Your angels loved to draw in the sky. Children are open to this energy so maybe that is the reason they can spot the best cloud pictures.

If your angels reach for you, you might notice a silhouette of an angel in a cloud. Or you might find other symbolism. These are some of the most commonly drawn cloud pictures by angels.

Dreams

There are times when we simply aren't open for angelic communication during the day. This is something that happens to everyone, even people who have trained to be more attuned and open to angelic communication. Sometimes we feel too exhausted, too stressed, and our souls get too weary.

This is what your angels get. They understand that sometimes, they will need to wait until you aren't distracted from earthly life to communicate with them. They are often at your side in dreams.

Dreaming of angels is an obvious sign that they are communicating to you. However, they also use dream states to relay messages that may not seem so obvious. Did you dream of finding the answers to your problems? Are you having trouble with something? Did you have a dream that made you feel relieved? You may have had a dream about certain elements that stood out and you encountered those elements the next day. If so, you're probably familiar with the process of communicating with your angels.

Numbers

How many times did you wonder if there was a way to win millions in the lottery by noticing a repeating pattern in numbers? While numbers patterns may not be the best way to make your own fortune, they can lead you to blessings.

If you see a sequence of numbers or numbers repeating, it is a sign your angels are in touch. When I notice this, I ask myself if it is meaningful. Sometimes there is. Sometimes there aren't. When there is, the message is clear to me and I need to pay attention. When there isn't, they acknowledge and thank me and I then pay attention throughout the day. They could be saying hi or they might be telling me that I need to be more alert and sensitive to energy.

Any repeated number can signify your angels. However repetitions of one or three are stronger signs of angelic communication.

Touching Sensation. Sudden Chills. Warmth

Perhaps you felt that someone touched your shoulder but then no one was there. A sudden drop in temperature without any explanation? Your angels can cause random, unexplained phenomena.

Angels are not capable to interact physically with us, in the same manner that we interact. They can not hug us or hold our hands in the traditional human sense.

We experience a strong surge of energy when angels attempt physical interaction with us. You might feel someone touch you or the surge could be more generalized like a temperature change. A sudden goose bump or shudder that goes unanswered are other physical signs your angels are greeting you.

Orbs

Orbs are little flashes and balls of floating light used by angels to travel between realms.

You are most likely to see your angel if there is flashing or shining light out of one corner of your eye. If you see scattered spots of light or color in your eye, it could mean you need an exam. However, this could also indicate that you have an angel.

Orbs are often so flashy that we don't even notice them. Sometimes, though we may be able to capture their quick movements. This happens when you get the shot at just the right moment. I find it fascinating that images with family and children are more likely contain orbs. It is our visual proof to the world that our angels are always present. When we gather, this angelic energy becomes even stronger.

Bells

It was not common for bells to ring throughout the day in the past. Bells are no longer used and collected in the same manner as they were in old towns clocks. This makes it even more important when we hear them.

Bells are often used for heavenly and angelic symbolism. A bell's simple tonal and resonant sound instantly raises the vibration where it is occurring. This opens up communication channels between us and our angels.

Listen to the bells ringing if you can. What is your immediate reaction? Does anything immediately come to your head? If you're given a bell, you can treat it as an extra special blessing. Feel more connected with your angels by ringing it whenever you wish.

Direct Messages

Sometimes messages from our angels aren't cryptic or hidden. Sometimes they appear right in our face, plain and simple.

Angels want to communicate with our hearts by making us pay more attention to the direct messages that are being sent around us. Consider a billboard you notice every day, a book you find at the library that grabs at you at random, or a headline you see in a newspaper or magazine you aren't usually interested in.

I remember a couple with young children who were experiencing a difficult time. They were walking along the street on one of the darkest days. They started to notice things. One noticed that people were wearing messages such as "Just breath" and "You Got This" on their shirts. The other noticed that there was a vanity license plate with the words "blessings of you" along other very strong messages. These shirts and license plates were not created by angels. But they placed them in the couple's path so that they could be noticed.

Music

Music raises a room's vibrational energies. When possible, I use music to facilitate communication with my angels. Sometimes, the angels use music to communicate.

Certain music helps us to be more open to the angelic energies. Music composed for meditation, spiritual services or other purposes is an example. Our angels know we are all unique and that not everyone responds to the same music. It doesn't matter if the song or type of music you like makes you feel closer to your angels, so don't ignore it.

Beauty: A Reality

This is one way that angels can communicate to us. This is about taking ordinary things and suddenly making them extraordinary.

It's your angel communicating with you when you walk through your community and see the beauty in something that you have already seen a hundred times.

If you find yourself going through a hard time and suddenly feel grateful for it and see the beauty in the situation, this is your angel.

You can hear your angel telling you that your problems are suddenly turned into blessings.

Your angels wish you to see the beauty of the process. They realize that what we are experiencing here is only temporary. What lies on either side is beauty we can only imagine.

They can help us see the beauty of our lives, making it easier and more pleasurable.

Someone Reaching out to You

Sometimes angels have very specific messages to send to us. They don't always get it across because we aren't ready to receive them. When they are unable or unwilling to reach us, they will assign the task of reaching someone else.

You can tell that angelic influence is evident by receiving a call or text from someone you haven't heard from for a while. Angels whisper in someone's ear so you hear the message you need.

Angels may also be working when you feel the sudden urge to reach out. I believe it is a sign that your heart is open to the possibility of something being said, and it shouldn't be hidden. It might just be an angel whispering in you ear.

Scent

Angels communicate with our hearts using all of their senses. One sense that is often forgotten about is our sense of taste.

Angels are typically associated with a sweet scent, but sometimes it can be floral. These are only some of the more common instances. If you have a pleasant lingering smell that isn't obvious, give it a chance and tell your angel.

Earrings

As a kid, I was taught that if your ears ring, you are either being thought about or spoken about. I still think about this every single time my ears rings. Now, I am open-minded to the possibility that it may not be another human, but my angels.

I've often mentioned how an angelic presence can shift the vibrations in a space. Our bodies will respond, even though it might not be obvious to us. When we feel a ringing inside our ears, it is a sign our bodies are responding.

Feeling As if You Are Not Alone

I will admit that it was initially a bit unsettling. It can be uncomfortable to feel as though you are alone and that no one is there for you. Having said that, I now feel attuned and able to sense when my angels support me.

This is where intuition comes in. There will be times where you feel uncomfortable with this presence. If you feel truly uncomfortable, place yourself in a bubble and ask for the help of your angels. The presence of your angels can make you feel more comfortable. If you don't feel the right feeling after asking, your angels might be warning you. You can take note of where you are and move around if necessary.

Someone Calls Your Name

Another sign of your angels can feel a little strange the first few times you hear it. This is when someone calls your name and you don't know anyone else.

This is a good way to grab attention from your angels. It's more than a greeting from your angels. Listen carefully when you hear your name. Is there something you should pay close attention to in your immediate surroundings? Could the solution to something you've struggled with suddenly be right before your eyes?

Children and pets

When we are born, our spirit world is fresh and we feel a deep connection to it. Children are able to see through the veil from six to eight years old. Children are more comfortable communicating with others when they are young, because they don't know how to ignore it. Young children may appear to smile or speak with another person.

This doesn't necessarily mean they are engaging in imaginative play.

Animals, because they are pure spirits, also act in this way. They are extremely sensitive to changes in energie and will respond to even the slightest shifts.

What you need, when and where you need it

I'm going to end my discussion by mentioning the concrete symbol of angelic communication. Your angels will make sure you have what you need, and that it is truly yours.

I know. We have all experienced those moments. Maybe your utility company sent you a disconnection notice and the money didn't show up. Maybe someone refused to provide assistance. Maybe you simply needed some positivity but only got rain and clouds. I get it. I have been there. I've also been able look back on these moments to realize that I really had everything that I needed.

I learned to use my resources when the bill didn't come through. I learned more from myself when I needed help and didn't receive it. I also learned humility. I learned to see beauty in the darkness when I needed the sun and got the rain. I am able to look back and recall many times when the solution appeared, and how it came into my hands. I trust the process and have learned to trust that my angels remain with me just as they are with all of you.

Strengthening Your Relationship to the Angelic Realm

All relationships take work and time. Your relationship is the same with your angels.

Even though your angels will always be there for your needs, they won't leave you until you work hard to make your connection stronger.

The process of strengthening your connection to the angelic realm can be both straightforward and difficult. It's easy because the angels are waiting for your call. But, it's challenging because there are many emotional barriers you need to break down before the connection can take place.

It is not difficult at all. The rest is easy. Recognizing your angels presence daily is the best thing to do to strengthen your connection. There are many ways to accomplish this. Here are some ways that I enjoy strengthening my connection to my angels. You can use any combination of them, or none at all. It is entirely up to you. It is important to begin somewhere. You might find that your angelic connection will strengthen as you put into practice a few more of these techniques.

When something becomes routine, it is more likely that you will develop a habit. A commitment to exercising at the same time each day will make it easier for you to stick to your exercise routine. Friends are more likely join you for weekly coffee if there is a fixed time and date. Your angels will love you for planning when to communicate. Pick a day and time that you can connect with your guardian, angels. Choose one day each week to connect with angelic beings such the archangels as well as your spirit guides.

When it comes to receiving messages of your angels, you should keep your mind open and your heart open. You never know what angels might be trying to get in touch with you. If your mind is closed off, it's possible to miss the message. Also, it shows your angels you are willing and able to work together to improve the connection. You might find that they start communicating more often with you.

* Keep images about angels around your car, house, and work. This could include a photograph, a small figurine, or a symbol representing angels, such as an image of a rainbow or feather.

* Consider an angel oracle deck. They are similar to tarot decks, but have completely different uses. You can choose an angel that you would like to connect with and take that card with you or pick up a card daily for angelic guidance.

* Do not expect your angels or guides to solve all your problems. Some people like to try and prove their theory that their angel will always help them by becoming recklessly irresponsible. This not only shows angels that your aren't respectful of them, but also tells them that they don't respect you. Angels cannot interfere with your free will. It's unfair to place that burden upon them. Be a conscious thinker and do your best to promote spiritual growth.

* When you are faced with a problem or are in a difficult situation, don't blame others or get angry. Instead, seek out your angels for solutions. I find myself asking "Why" almost every day. I try to make it a habit of looking in the right direction.

* Write a letter to heaven every week. Write down everything you want to send to your angels. But you don't really have to send it, as the cost of postage is prohibitive. Once you've written it down, it is much simpler to release it into angelic space. A ritual in which the letter is lit over a pure-white candle can also be used to release the energy into spiritual realms.

Invite your angels. When you go to bed at night, say a prayer. Then invite your angels to join in on your dreams. This allows your angels to know that you are open for communication. It also allows communication to be initiated at a time you are most open for interaction between realms.

* Just repeat it. Talk to your angels. This is the simplest and most effective way to strengthen your connections: just initiate the conversation. Your angels are always here for you and want to communicate with. Give them the chance and they will.

* Be open for solutions and ideas that may not have otherwise occurred to your. Sometimes our angels leave us baffled by a message. It might seem completely unexpected. Give credit to your angels and give them some credit for their advice. They see the world from a different perspective than you. They have insight that you don't. Try it even if you find it crazy. You'll probably be pleasantly surprised.

* Listen to the guidance you receive. It makes your angels feel validated when you do things that make them feel loved. You have already taken the first step by being open and receptive. Now you can take the next step and act on their advice.

* Finally, remember to be thankful every day. Gratitude is a sure method to attract more blessings. Do you feel more inclined to help someone when you know they are grateful than when you don't? Angels are not dependent on gratitude. However, they do appreciate it. Recognizing them is an act of

gratitude. By acknowledging their presence, you can strengthen the relationship between you two.

The most important thing is to have patience as you work towards strengthening your connection and building a friendship with your angels. It takes more than just one attempt. You wouldn't ask someone for lunch only once and expect them not to be your best friends. There's still so much you can learn about your partner and how to nurture that relationship. Take your time, and let the experience unfold.

Under the Protection of Angels

Many see this as a fallen world full of pain and danger. There will come a time in each of our lives when we require additional protection. In these instances, protection may be required for our heart, physical safety, well-being, and soul.

There are times when it is necessary to experience difficult or scary situations as part of our journey. Many people experience the difficult times alone.

There is a difference in how angels protect people when they are helping you with difficult or necessary tasks and how they protect those who have been sent to protect them. The first type is nurturing, healing protection. The second is interference that prevents/protects you in a potentially dire situation. Remember that your angels will not interfere with you free will. There is a limit to their abilities. They may be capable of intervening and preventing an accident, but they cannot do anything for someone who deliberately chooses to behave recklessly.

There is a fine line in between the times when angels naturally protect you, and when you need it. Free will is an important part of this equation. It is therefore a good idea that you ask for protection every day as well as whenever special circumstances arise that will provide extra protection for your or others. Even though you don't need to do any kind of ritual or prayer to ask for protection (many people love the energy that comes from ritual), it is not necessary. Simply send a prayer and ask. It doesn't make a difference where you are asking, what you ask, or how it is done. It does not matter how you ask or what you do.

Your angels offer protection in two ways: spiritual protection and protection physically.

Spiritual Protection

Your guardian angels protect you from all the negative and dark energies that are part of the spiritual world. Because everyone has their own spiritual philosophies, I won't be too detailed about the "evil" out there. It doesn't matter what beliefs you have, there can be negative effects on your spiritual health if they aren't addressed.

The archangel Michael (or warrior angel) is considered to be the leader of negative forces. Michael's direction directs your guardian Angels to defeat negative forces. Their goal is to prevent negative energies from impacting your life.

When negative or dark energies are trying to attack, it is common to feel the effects on our mental or emotional outlook. When negative energy has become too powerful for our spiritual well-being, we can feel depressed, anxious, afraid, or hopeless.

I do not deny the fact that mental problems can have physical causes. But, sometimes these feelings can be caused by our inability to receive angelic interference. Remember that part about divine intervention as well as free will? Without an invitation or your explicit permission, there are limits to the protection that angels can provide for you.

If you find yourself in an emotionally dark place, or you feel spiritually under attack and need protection, ask your angels. If you feel in need of protection, give your angels the green light to do so. You can ask for their help by praying, affirming or performing a ritual. You can also ask

"Archangel Michael. Please send my guardian wardens to protect myself from the dark and destructive energies of this universe. Thank you.

Protect your body

Your guardian or angels' other task is to protect your from all forms of physical harm, so long as they don't interfere with your spiritual or personal will. If you happen to be in an unsafe place or at the wrong moment, your guardian angel can help you avoid a serious car accident. If it is part or a learning experience, the angel may also be there to help you.

This concept is hard for most people. Most people think that any bad thing that happens is a sign that our guardian or angels are failing to perform their duties, or worse still, that we don't have any angels.

Even though they may not seem to be there, even though you feel alone, angels are always there for your protection. If you feel that your angels have let you down, take a few moments to ask them why. Your answer might not be clear, but you will get it eventually if they pay attention. Your angels want your understanding and will help you heal from any trauma, illness or pain you have suffered.

It doesn't matter what kind of protection you need, this ritual is what I use to invoke their protective energy. This little ritual shows your angels that you are open to their protective energies. You are allowing your angels to protect you. These are Divinely-planned events that are part and parcel of the soul's path. You can ask for their guidance and receive their healing, loving energy. This will keep you from falling into a worse place.

Ritual for Protection in the Archangel Michael

The archangel Michael acts as the strongest protector among the archangels. This ritual requires us to call on Michael specifically to ask him to be there and to send angels around to protect and surround us. This ritual is perfect for protecting yourself against any type of danger, but it can be particularly helpful against "soulleaches", who stick to you and drain your energy. It is difficult for emergency protection to be used because it is a ritual. If you're in an emergency, don't fret about setting the scene and formalities. Call the archangel Michael immediately and ask for protection.

Now, for the ritual.

Find a quiet area where you can unassistedly sit and enjoy the silence. Spend a few seconds relaxing and quieting the mind.

As your mind settles, imagine a brilliantly blue blanket beneath you that covers the entire ground. Imagine the blanket rolling along the ground and reaching as far out as you can.

Call to Michael the Archangel and ask him to surround you with his protective energy.

Imagine a blue blanket that wraps around you. You can move freely inside it, but no one can enter it without your permission.

Imagine this blanket as a cloak-like covering for your head and stretching down to your toes. As the blanket wraps your body, you feel grounded to the earth below.

Do it again:

"Divine Protection surrounds me so I can't be hurt."

You will continue this process many times until your confidence is restored.

Now, say this prayer to thank Michael the Archangel Michael for his protection.

Thank you Angel of God for keeping watch over me as my walk this earth. I ask that you protect me. I also request that you send more angels whenever necessary to be faithful protectors and watchful over me and those I love.

Be confident that you are protected and watched over by your angels.

Healing Angels

Through energy transformation, angels are able to heal us. Pure energy makes us all. This energy flows freely when you are healthy. Sometimes this energy is blocked. There are many types of illness and distress that can occur when this happens.

Blockage can lead to physical illnesses and is often the source of emotional distress. You may experience fear, anger and distrust. Angels can help us break down these blocks and allow the energy of balance to flow through our bodies.

Two methods are available for you to reach the healing powers of your angels. The first option is to simply inquire about them. Simply asking your angels for help is enough. Another option is to consult an angelic healer. These are people who are attuned for angelic energy. Some people feel that angelic healers increase their energy vibration, while others feel it is too personal to trust someone else. Your angels are available to assist you, no matter your circumstances. All you have to do is to ask. They will reach you via the most comfortable means.

You may be wondering if angels can help with healing. The short answer? Your angels can deal with all kinds of healing requests from anxiety to serious disease and everything in-between. The long answer is not the only one.

You likely have a very specific plan when you reach out to your angels for help, especially if a loved is going through a difficult or life-threatening situation. You may call your angels seeking healing energy. The results you receive might leave you feeling abandoned or betrayed.

It's important to recognize that there are things both that are divine and things free from will. If you've been in an accident and need to speed up healing, your angels are there to help. Your angels may recognize your need to help with any kind of illness. This is especially true if it involves the preparation of the body for the return to the spiritual plane. You can have these transformations made easier by angels, although they cannot interfere with your divine will.

One last thing: Angels cannot be considered doctors. Angels can heal on an energetic basis. They cannot heal a wound or administer medicine that can fight most of the illnesses they come across. We often forget that our operation is in a different realm than angels. While we can reach out and connect with them, they are not able to transform our health in the exact same way as modern medicine. If you have a medical emergency, seek help and then ask for the assistance of your angels.

These are the reasons why you should ask your Angels for healing

Your Angels do not specialize; they can help with all your needs

Your angels can send you healing energy for all kinds of sicknesses, injuries, and ailments, whether they are spiritual, emotional, or physically. They are pure and loving energy, and can focus that energy where it is needed. It is your free will to choose, so do not be upset at your angels for not intervening. You must let them know that your intention is to help their healing energies.

Being willing and open to your Angels' Healing Energy can help you along the right path

Sometimes, emotional and physical illnesses can occur because we haven't been on the right path for spiritual growth. The truth that is in alignment with your soul will cause you to drift off track and create blockages in your energy field.

Your angels will have a unique perspective about your life. They have access the universal knowledge, truths and wisdom. This allows them the ability to simultaneously view the future, present, past and current. Only the ability of seeing clearly past and present is possible, but it's difficult to assess the current situation accurately. What do you think would happen to your perception if you could see the future ahead? Sometimes the seemingly insurmountable circumstances in our lives won't seem so awful suddenly. Instead of reacting to fear and making quick decisions, we might reflect and decide on loving ourselves.

Your angels can assist you with this. When you call for healing, they will use their knowledge to guide the healing in a way best suited to your life path.

They amplify the natural healing process in sleep

It is obvious that good sleep is crucial for your well-being. Your body uses the sleep time to repair, detoxify, and rejuvenate. Sleep is the best "medicine" to use when you feel tired, sick, or just plain unwell.

Angels love to be with us during the most open times for their energy. Not surprisingly, their favorite time to connect with us is when they are asleep. The dream state provides a natural way for communication. When you're sleeping, you can pray to your angels for healing.

They find and fix the real source of your distress

Modern medicine has many options that can help us relieve our symptoms or to address the real cause of our distress. Although you may be able take an over the counter medication to ease your allergy headaches, it won't change how your body reacts. Your symptoms may be relieved by a cough medicine, but the treatment will not cure your condition. Sometimes we just need to feel better while the body heals. Sometimes we need to address the root cause of the distress so that it heals.

Angels work on an energetic level to heal those who call. They don't simply magically disappear your symptoms. This means that your illness or blockage will be healed or cleared, even if it is not obvious. Your angels may be more than just soothing your allergy headaches. Many health issues have emotional causes. A sore back, for instance, could indicate that you are feeling disconnected. You might have laryngitis if you don't listen to your inner voice. Your angels are able to recognize these issues and work with you in healing them.

Angelic healing is soothing in times of stress

Many people, me included, experience anxiety when an illness strikes. Perhaps the stomach bug is causing stress in your life. It is possible that you are worried about the future of your loved ones or yourself.

It is common to be left in these situations wondering how we will pay our bills if we miss a day of work. Who will watch my kids if it's impossible to get out of bed? How will this illness impact my quality-of-life? How will my loved one recover?" Some of these questions are easy to answer, others may require soul-searching and introspection. These questions cause stress and anxiety which can be particularly detrimental to someone who's already in a poor state of health.

Chapter 5 Healing through the Archangel Raphael

Raphael (the archangel Raphael) is full of powerful, loving, healing energy. He will always answer your call if you ask. For times of emotional and physical distress, I love the following prayer and ritual to connect with Raphael.

As a reminder, you may call Raphael the archangel Raphael to seek healing for someone close to. But, it is best to ask their permission. Raphael can only offer the amount of healing energy that they are open to receiving without their consent.

The color green is a strong symbol of Raphael and I like to use it in my ritual. This is up to the individual and is not mandatory.

Find somewhere quiet enough to sit for a while.

Take a few deep inhalations and concentrate on the areas of concern you have regarding the health of yourself or others.

As you sit there, your heart will beat very strongly. It is a steady, strong rhythmic beat. This soothes you.

Imagine a gentle, healing green light swirling around you. This is your heart chakra. It's located in the center of your upper chest.

As this green light swirls through your heart chakra it grows stronger until it reaches the rest of your body.

Allow it to reach all cells of your body, stretching along every finger or toe until no part is left unhealed by this healing energy.

Now say this:

"Archangel Raphael. With you, as a vessel. May the divine energy and love flow through (or to) me, and heal me.

This process can be repeated until you begin to feel the healing power of your energy as it pulses through.

As a physical sign of willingness and readiness to be infused with healing energy, lift your arms towards the heavens.

Thanks to Raphael the archangel for his presence.

This ritual is not closed. You may continue your day or night as usual, allowing healing energy to flow through you body.

You can continue repeating the affirmation until you feel the need to strengthen your body's healing abilities.

Another prayer I like to use is when I need to heal or have someone that allows me to pray on their behalf to the angels. It is as follows:

"Glorious Raphael, the healing prince from the heavenly court. May you bless me with wisdom, love, safety, and protection.

I ask you for your help in alleviating my sufferings. You are welcome to come and help me lift the burden of my past while also healing the ailments that have affected me in this lifetime.

I come to your aid humbly, asking for your healing and guidance for me and all those who are greatly affected by the world's suffering.

Amen."

Yes, it is something I've repeated many times. However, it is important that I reiterate it. It's not just about how you ask the angels for their help. All you need to do is ask. Period.

May you be surrounded by angels and loved ones during all your life's trials, and may the archangel Raphael help you to ease your tired spirit and body whenever you are in pain.

Living a Life Guided and Directed by Angels

We've covered a lot in this book about who your angels can be and how you can reach out to them during times when you have a special need. But, what we haven't talked about much is living a life guided in part by your angels. What I mean is the routine, ordinary days. How can we invite angels and receive their presence every day of the week?

How can you honor your angels? Make small, daily rituals to show your appreciation and love them.

You can start by asking yourself these questions.

Are there ways I can easily see how my life is meaningful each morning as I wake-up?

Do I have the ability to find joy in my own life and feel a real sense of excitement about every day?

Do you feel that your life has purpose and that every day brings you closer to reaching your full potential?

Do I have a strong intuition? Do I trust my inner voice more than external guidance and advice?

Do I be true to me? Am I being honest and authentic?

Did I learn to put aside the opinions of others?

What have I done to learn to be open to forgiveness?

Do I have goals, and do I have a plan? Are my goals clear and do I have a plan?

Are I spiritually connected to others? Are you able to look at others and see the connection?

Do I consider spiritual growth essential? Do I place it as a top priority, or does it remain on the sidelines?

Do I recognize self-limiting behaviors and thoughts? Do I know how they can be released?

Do I feel connected and in touch with my angels Do I feel at ease asking for help, wisdom, and love?

If you answered yes, or almost all of these questions, then your angels are already guiding you. You are aware they are around and know how they can help you navigate each day and every new stage of life.

The other side is that if you answered no to all or most of these questions you still have the opportunity to learn more about how to invite your angels into your lives on a daily basis, and attune your energies to them.

Forgetting and building walls

When we begin to doubt our relationship with the angels it is important that we remember that the only things that stand between us and them can be those that we put in place.

Once upon an time, we had a relationship with the angels from the spiritual plane. When we agreed to a life here on Earth, we cut ourselves off from the more intimate relationships. We did this not out a lack of desire, but out a necessity. We cannot have the required experiences on this Earth while keeping the knowledge of God's spiritual world.

The process of forgetting and seperating at birth began. Every day thereafter, time became an ever-growing obstacle in keeping the connection to the angels. Time is a factor in our forgetting. This is true for almost all things, even those we cherish most. We may retain lingering memories but we lose more of the experience with each passing day.

Our connection to the spiritual realm is replaced by logic, reason, and groundedness in the material world. Some things, such an open conversation with the angels or a simple relationship with them, that we once found so natural suddenly seem bizarre, or even insane. Each day, reason is stronger and logic becomes more sophisticated until we begin to doubt that the angelic realm exists apart from the creative mind.

Your childhood faith or affiliation can influence your approach to angels and their realm. Some see them merely as messengers of God. Others see them as close friends or more intimate. Others don't acknowledge their existence.

Your angels never leave your side, no matter your belief level. They don't require that you believe in their existence. They need your permission and acknowledgement to guide you or protect you at times. If you fail to make an effort, your relationship with the angels won't suffer. It will only grow stronger if we do.

Steps to a life guided by angels

While it may not always feel like that, I understand that we weren't meant to suffer. We're here to do many different things, but suffering continuously is not one. We are here as learners, to grow, as well to fulfill our purpose and be of service. Even if you do everything alone, it can be hard to reach those goals. You can connect to your angels to help you stay away from negative energies, self-destructive thoughts, and other things that could get in the way of your purpose. To live a life ruled by angels, you must open yourself up to them.

Each of our hearts opens up and allows us to connect with the spiritual realm. The many ways angels can connect with us is something you might not know. The following are some of the many ways that we can communicate with our angels:

* Prayer

* Ritual

* Meditation

* Visualization

* Listening for our intuition

* Connection to animals and nature

* Writing, such as letters and journals

* An appreciation for art

This is not an exhaustive list. There is no wrong way to communicate with your angels. They are always nearby and waiting for your connection in whatever way makes sense to you. They want to show love and support that resonates with you, so that your belief and connection to them is stronger.

If you are in a position in life where you want stronger connections and to welcome them into your lives, you already know the answer. It is only when you reach a place where you want to strengthen your connection and get more involved that you can recognize that you have to open up to their ever-loving and guiding energy.

There are some steps you can follow to have your life powered by angelic influence. These steps will not be the same as those to connect with your angels. It might be easier to explain these differences through the lens of real-life interactions. You can learn to communicate with your angels in a similar way to a couple who seeks therapy to develop a more open and honest dialogue. The work you need to do to learn how to live a life guided only by angels is similar to what you would do to make yourself an equal partner in your relationship. Before you can start improving your communication skills, first make sure that you are an equal partner.

I hate the idea of people thinking this is difficult. True, it's challenging at times. It is not uncommon for any spiritual development work to be hard at times. I know from experience that the more complex a process is, the more people are likely to abandon it and quit before it is finished. The act of living an angel guided life has been broken down into five steps. Some people can complete the steps in a few short days. For others it might take weeks to complete the process. You don't have to be discouraged if this takes longer. Of course, the more we put into something, often the result is more rewarding. Trust your process and work at a pace that suits your needs.

Step one: You must start by creating your own energy vibrations

Angels communicate energy to us. You might find someone you meet on the street who speaks a foreign language. This would cause you to have difficulty communicating. You can see energy as a language other than English: Your angels' language.

A way to describe positive energy by your "vibration"? Negative or dark energies vibrate at an extremely low level, while the positive vibrates at higher levels. The closer an energy is to pure, loving love, the stronger its vibration. Not only does it open up the possibility of communication but it also helps to shield you from much negativity. Low-functioning negative energies cannot penetrate higher vibrational energy. You are creating a protective energy field around your self.

These are just a few ways to boost your vibrational level.

* Meditate. Meditate.

* Take note of the beauty around yourself. Once you start to notice the beauty, there is less room for the ugly. It is possible to replace every negative idea with a positive thought over time.

* Give and receive love. Don't be afraid to give compliments to strangers.

* Detox your life. All types of detox can be considered here. Get rid of all the junk food and toxic people in your life.

* Learn to be a good listener. It is hard to feel drained or overburdened faster than feeling depleted and exhausted. Be realistic about your obligations to other people. Ask yourself what might happen if someone said no. Do you think the world would end? No. Is it possible for them to become upset or irritable? Maybe. Maybe they could understand. Maybe. Does it really matter? In

most cases, no. You have an obligation towards some people in your lives, but it's important to respect your limits and set boundaries. This will keep you positive and your energy high. This might be a good time to add the person to the detox. See above.

* Water, water, everywhere. Water is cleansing. Feeling clean makes it easier to receive angelic guidance. Get a relaxing bath with Epsom Salt or a refreshing dip in the ocean. Let Mother Nature's salty seawater soothe, cleanse, and recharge you.

* Get moving regularly. You can't have energy if you aren't moving. A stalled physique is not good. It is important to move your body every day, at whatever level you feel most comfortable. You can move your arms and legs with ease, or dance freely to get that energy flowing.

Step Two: Talk to your Angels!

This book covers all of it. Start applying what you have learned so that you can communicate with your angels.

Step Three - You are here because you have a purpose. What is it?

Your angels will help you. Did you ever try to help someone who was lost? Only to find that they didn't know the way to get there? When there is no destination, it is impossible for someone to find their way. Remember that you have complete freedom of choice. You cannot expect your angels to simply pick up you and lead you down a path that you do not wish to follow.

Being guided by angels is about finding your destination. Ask them for assistance if you are having trouble finding your direction or purpose. Don't assume they will choose it for your. This is work that must be done.

Step Four: Identify Your Obstacles

This is another situation that angels can assist you in, but this time you will have to do all the work. Is there anything preventing or hindering you from living the life that you want? It is important to examine this question in depth. You should look at both positive aspects and negative aspects. Sometimes, what appears to be a positive thing can actually be quite restrictive. Obstacles could include people, jobs. thoughts, emotions, or anything else that might hinder you from living your truest life, with the guidance and support of your angels.

Once you've identified the obstacles, make a plan to eliminate them. While there are some roadblocks that can be overcome, others may not be so difficult. The problem is that many of these roadblocks are unsolved. You will encounter the roadblock each time you attempt to go down that path. Eliminating the obstacle will allow you to travel in your own way, free of stress or worry.

Step 5: Join your Team

Now is the time to do the preliminary work. You know the direction that you want to take in your life and you have removed any obstacles. You have taken steps in raising your energy vibrations to make you more open and receptive towards your angels' guidance. For the angels' assistance, you just need to extend your hand.

Your angels will assist you in navigating those turns; they will direct you along the most efficient path. How can angels be thanked for their help? Their only request is that you be authentic and kind towards all people. There is no need to make sacrifices in order to say thank you to your angels. All you have to do is to acknowledge them, to listen to them, to thank them for their contributions to your life.

The special relationship between Angels and Children

Because the angel-child relationship is so beautiful and pure, I thought it was important to include it in this book. There is much discussion about how children can be more open to the spiritual realm. It is believed that children can see spirit guides and angels better than adults. I believe this to true.

Children are so young that they have never seen the earth before. They are also closer to the universal truths they once knew before they were born into the world.

Children don't yet have a strong sense of logic and reasoning. Children do not automatically conclude that seeing an angel means they are imagining or going insane. Spiritual beings are part of their daily life.

If you have a child who is special and thinks they are communicating with angels, then your suspicions may be true. Parents and other adults who are involved in the child's lives might be concerned that their imaginations have gone too far. There are some signs that your child might be interacting with angels. Some people may worry that their child might be interfacing with negative emotions. This would not be something to worry about. Some adults may find communication from the spiritual world disturbing. They will also associate it negatively with "supernatural" connotations. I would love to calm your fears if you are one of these people.

Your child has angels just like you. They are there as a guide, protector, and lover for the child. Sometimes, they might become a little playful and interact a lot with the child. It is possible for them to play with you, if you're open to it. The angelic energy surrounding a child is always filled by heavenly light. There is absolutely nothing to be worried about if a child mentions talking to or playing with an angel.

Conversely, children can be influenced by the same negative influences that adults are. If you care for a child, you must be alert for shifts in energy. But don't worry too much. It's acceptable to call upon the angels to guard your child if you feel there is negative energy.

While an adult must openly and willingly receive angelic energy to make your call work, children are still under the control of adults. Angels understand that children need to be guided and protected, especially when the child is too young.

These are some signs that you can trust angels to guide, love and care for your child.

They have imaginary buddies

Many imaginary friends are not angels. Children can make anything seem real to them if they have an imagination. They may have trouble distinguishing between the real and imagined events. You might see them come in after playing outside and talk about what they did with the flowers, or how they made imaginary friends to play in the sandbox. Their imaginations can be so wild that all they see seems real. Do you remember listening to a child tell you about their imaginary adventures as you sat there? These things are real to them.

Sometimes, their imaginations are more real than what they actually see. As long as your child has a reliable imaginary friend, be sure to ask as many as questions as you can without being pushy or chastising. Ask the friend their name, how they look and what they like doing. Most of the time, at least one answer will be given to these questions. This is a sure sign you child is in the company of angels.

They feel the presences of angels

Every encounter a child has, with their angels, will not be in the form a imaginary friend. Children are open-minded and receptive to angels. They haven't been taught to associate them only with the human form. Children are more inclined to feel or sense their angels then adults. Sometimes a child may become obsessed with a particular color. He or she might talk about seeing clouds of that colour, or dreaming about that color. If this happens, it is possible that they are picking up on the color energy associated each angel.

Angels' loving energy is also more accessible to children. Because angels are surrounding them, a child might suddenly feel very warm and fuzzy. They may associate sounds of bells ringing as feelings of love, contentment, and joy.

They come with an inherent safety net

Do you ever wonder how children can survive even in the most dire situations? It's amazing how children can take a tumble but, despite being afraid they might hurt themselves, they will bounce back and be fine.

Yes, children are more resilient when they are younger. The angels of childhood are busy, running around to cushion falls and move objects out of the way. They also hold children up safe as they explore.

Their wishes are fulfilled

As an adult, there are likely many things you would like to do. I would guess that only a few of these wishes come to pass. You can either work for the thing you want or request help from someone else to make it happen. I cannot count how many times a day I wished for more happiness or more resources. These things weren't going to magically be bestowed on me. Instead, I had the to open up to more avenues for abundance. I had also to learn how get a good sleep. Children, on the contrary, are much more blessed when they wish.

Do you remember a time when a child wished for a certain toy, but was too costly for you? Only to discover it on sale or a gently used model in your possession? Imagine your child wishing to see a close friend or relative and then seeing that person suddenly appear on the doorstep. Angels love to grant children wishes because fulfilled wishes equal potential. Children are full with wishes. A child with a wish granted every now-and-then might be more likely believe in the beauty around the world, and will share love and light.

Be assured that your child's angels won't grant all your wishes. You don't need to worry about whether your child will be spoilt by their angels and if you will miraculously get tickets to Disney. There are bounds, and the angels wish to bring joy in ways that help your child become a caring, nurturing adult.

When your child is talking about an imaginary friend or telling a story so complex that it is hard not to believe they are making it up, take a moment to listen. What you're seeing is the very real and strong connection between children, their angels. It is one such beautiful angelic relationship that you might ever come across. Take a deep breath and reflect. Children have a lot to teach us about opening our hearts to the spirit realm.

History of the Archangels

It is helpful to have a basic understanding of the meanings and origins of words and phrases over the past several centuries in order to fully understand the phenomena of archangels. Many people interpret angels or archangels as Christians in the west. This could be as simple or as simple as the image above of cherubic baby angels sitting on clouds and playing their harps. It could be those who serve God and do God's bidding. It can even think of abstract and difficult ideas that go against all common reality. To fully understand the Christian interpretation, and the modern archangels as well as the role of angels throughout Abrahamic religions, it is important to also look at the role of angels. Islam, Judaism (and Christianity) all present their own versions of the angelic ranks to this world. But what information do we need about the history religious archangels'?

The word archangel, etymologically speaking comes from Greek. The first word of the phrase, "arch," can be roughly translated by "chief," to indicate the specific angels' position in comparison with other angelic figures. Although most people are familiar enough with the concept angels, it is possible to view the archangels as a separate entity.

The archangels Michael and Gabriel are the most prominent in all three Abrahamic religions. Raphael sometimes joins these two figures, as they are mentioned throughout many of the books comprising the Bible, Quran, or Torah. As you look through the history and traditions of Christianity, you will find that there are many opinions about Raphael's inclusion in this exalted group. Islam also mentions Azrael Israfil and Judaism Metatron, which is an archangel.

Over the course religious history, our current interpretations of the archangels have changed markedly. One of the most widely held views is the pantheon of seven Archangels. This group is considered the most important. Along with Raphael Michael, Gabriel, Raphael, and Remiel the pantheon of seven archangels was also popularized by religious scholars. These figures (or at most, the mention of them in texts) are mentioned by the Bible. You can trace their lineage back the early church workers that helped develop many core principles of Christianity. Pope

Gregory I, later made Saint, leaves one among the first written clues concerning the seven angels. He makes the point of listing all the angels which he believes should belong in the category.

When we examine the history of the pantheon, we see that the names aren't always the same. Since so many cultures, societies, and religions are not able to agree on the identity or even seven of the archangels, it has taken centuries before our knowledge began to coalesce. Some may find it odd, however, that the modern view of archangels is so different from the historical narrative. The history of the beings can be viewed to confirm that they are not fixed. There is no correct or wrong history of the archangels. When dealing with spiritual beings such as archangels, there is a lot of potential for interpretation. While it helps to understand the different historical patterns of archangels we can also see that there is no correct answer. This book will demonstrate that you can harness the power the archangels yourself, and not just by reading the Quran or Torah. Instead, one should see the fact some of the world's most powerful religions hold the concept so close as their beliefs as a reflection in an inherent truth or quality in phenomena of the archangels.

Modern interpretations

Although the idea of archangels' power and existence has been around since many millennia ago, we now understand their capabilities and are beginning to harness them. Legends tell of magical practitioners who were able summon spirits and archangels from before Christ's birth. Numerous people claim that they have been able, through various shamans and priests working in temples with Solomon's keys or other means, to summon the archangels to assist them. These secrets were previously considered sacred information. However, modern researchers have tirelessly worked to open up the possibility of summoning archangels without you having to become a priest or magickal researcher.

Modern views of the archangels are a bit different. The belief is that archangels have an extraordinary power. They can access a portion of the grace that is held by higher beings as extensions of the greater divine presence. They can appear in many forms as they represent such a powerful and vital power. Their greatest skill is healing. They can take many forms as healers. They can carry out surgery on our wounded bodies, or they can help us heal from the pain of emotional trauma. They can hold the power and will of the Divine in their hands. They arrive on Earth as metaphysical forms and it can be difficult reaching out to touch them. However, the fact that they are present among us is a great comfort.

For those who have studied the Bible or other religious texts, you will be familiar with the concept of God. The archangels do not represent all of the power of God. If we believe a divine creator is an all-powerful omnipotent being who can do his bidding, then the archangels are many times more competent than mere humans. Archangels are truly powerful because of their ability to heal or mend.

Each person's approach to the archangels will be different. Some people invoke their spirits as part of a daily routine. Others pick and choose the times when they wish to call on the divine healers. You could find people turning to the archangels when in trouble or using the angels' protection power to protect them from future harm. There are no right or wrong ways to interact directly with the archangels. There are many ways to interact with the archangels, but some methods or practices can be more effective than others. The main tenant of modern faith in their existence is faith. The specific details of rituals and their effectiveness are irrelevant when it comes to faith. Faith is only as strong as the faith behind them. In modern archangels interpretations, it is often found that those who have the greatest faith are those who see best results.

So how can we feel the presence archangels are in our lives? For most people, even the strongest interactions are not obvious. A majority of people do not have the awareness or the willingness to extend their comprehension beyond the physical level. This can make it difficult for them to witness real magick in daily life. If the archangel chooses not to interact with such people they can often get through the episode unaware of what actually happened. They might forget that they received healing or other benefits as a result of the angel's benevolence. The angel does not care. This may seem unfair for those who wish to invoke the protection angels. But the goodness, and the divinity the archangels has the power to touch all. You will see that modern archangels' interpretations do not give you any control over these divine beings.

Instead, it can create a relationship that is mutually beneficial. When you are able to strengthen the relationship between yourself, the archangels and yourself, you will discover how rich, powerful, and rewarding it can be to invoke their power. Although we may not have the ability to control such powerful beings we can create a bond with them which increases our chances of understanding God. You can improve your spiritual well-being by learning the world of the Archangels.

Today, the existence of the archangels in the world of modern believers is less controversial than it was for Jewish, Christian, or Islamic theology. It is an opportunity to grow our knowledge of the Divine. It is a type of spirituality. The incantations and invocations you will learn later in this book will enhance your knowledge of the phenomenal and the metaphysical. Modern archangellore doesn't cater to those who want power and control. The modern world of archangels is a place where you can find self-improvement in life, happiness, protection, healing, and peace. Learning the special nature of the spiritual is just as important to one's self. It is common for those who have been involved in the archangel world to be happier and feel more at ease once they have increased their knowledge.

Now that we have an understanding of the role of archangels within modern society, we can start to understand how archangels will relate to us as individuals.

Chapter6 Roles and capabilities Archangels

This guide to archangels should give you a basic understanding of the potential power, ability and attributes of divine beings. It is not the truth that many people fully understand the abilities of the archangels. Although we have covered the historical and current conceptions of the archangels in this book, we did not discuss how they function with everyday life. This is the best chapter if you are looking to become involved in the world of archangels. In the pages that follow, we will discuss the ability of the archangels to influence, alter, and improve your lives.

Learning about archangels is the most important part of understanding them. The vast majority of people have a fixed view of human life and are unable to see the possibility of an angel. While most people can relate to and sympathize or imagine their friends, family, and even strangers, they cannot do the same with an angelic being. Their very nature makes it difficult for them to comprehend what it means being an archangel. It's quite different from being able understand your fellow human being.

So why is this so? Simply put, the divine natures the archangels have separates them from ours. We may share similarities with the Archangels but we are created by a higher power and are not the same. Anybody who has read Christian or Abrahamic literature will know that the legions if angels don't serve a purpose similar to ours is likely to be disappointed. They exist beyond Earth and transcend other planes, rather than just existing here. They do not have to deal in faith or belief matters, but their closeness with God is pre-arranged. Their ability, to understand and to wield this power as they travel between heaven & the mortal planes grants them power beyond our comprehension. Herein lies the problem. The world of an archangel is so vastly different, that a layman can only see the inside of their minds without having the right training and being willing to put faith into the paranormal.

This is the first hurdle people often encounter when learning about archangels. However, for those who desire to expand their knowledge of this mysterious plane and gain more insight into it, the act of opening this volume is a clear sign of the will and determination required to attract the power of angels to your life. If we are willing to acknowledge that angels/archangels exist as legitimate forces in the world, which is evident by reading this far, we can start to map and understand how they affect our daily lives.

As we discussed in the book, one important role that archangels perform in the world of angels is that of healers. The essential healing power of angelic power makes it one of the defining characteristics of angelic power. For most of the history organized religion has been about angels being a key link between humans and the Divine. They aid with communication and understanding the Creator. Their healing history goes far beyond being medical. Instead, they have been healing human relationships with God. Their healing qualities are vital to humanity's history. They can restore, guide and nurture human kindness, divinity, belief, and divinity. The pantheon, or angelic, can help us improve our philosophical, metaphysical, spiritual, and soulful well-being with the same skill that we might use to treat an injury or broken bone. Their healing power is multifaceted. They have one fundamental quality (healing), which can be demonstrated in a number of different ways.

This is one the most difficult aspects of the angels role. Even though their main responsibility lies in healing, there are many ways they do this. They could bring healing to the hurting or provide compassion to the poor. They might be guiding those who are unaware or lost. Their roles can seem abstract and obscure but they have a strong desire to make the world a better place. And that is where they come in. The power of the archangels can be invoked to bring a healing glow in your life. This can help to overcome challenges, solve issues, and deal with tricky situations.

Their powers can be extremely reactive. However, those who are best versed with the discourse of archangels may find themselves able to invoke the Divine beings preemptively to better protect themselves from any future threats. Being able to summon the protective and healing qualities of archangels before an event happens can be very useful for those who are concerned about your safety. They can help guide you and protect you against harm.

It is rare that people will ask for anything in return for the healing gifts they offer to the world. Like all matters of faith, belief is key. This book's advice is a great guideline. Those with the strongest faith will often achieve the best results. If you are able and willing to open your heart to the world of archangels, you will be able to build a stronger relationship with them. As with all beginner guides, there will be times when you may struggle. Despite this, it's crucial to keep faith in both the roles and healing powers of the legion if you are new to the world of archangels.

This chapter has primarily dealt with abstracts. This makes it very difficult to complete. The idea of healing is at the heart of the roles played by the archangels. Unfortunately, this property manifests in multiple ways so it can be difficult to point to physical results. Because angels are already present in many different realms of existence, it is sometimes difficult to pinpoint the exact location where they could legally function. People choose to interpret angels' existence as they would an exotic animal. However, empirical evidence is hard to find. An angel's healing powers rarely leave any mark. Rarely does it leave behind a permanent memory. It can, however, touch directly onto the soul and imprint their presence in the human condition. Some people reject this idea due to its metaphysical aspect.

However, people who deny the existence and healing abilities of archangels will not be exempted from them. While it might seem odd, some people believe that refusing belief in the Divine qualities these beings possess should not cause them to leave. Their role in the world is different. They serve as God's creatures and try to bring religion to the world. Even those who deny angels exist can receive healing spirits. While people who understand the relationship between humankind and the spiritual might be better equipped to make connections with angels or their likes, agnostics around the world are still welcome. Instead, the archangels are still able to reach out and heal people through their warm, glowing touch.

With this in mind let us now consider the role and capabilities of archangels. How does this affect our lives. How can they touch us? How can you tell when your soul has been touched by their presence?

Again, it is difficult to quantify. For those who've never met angelic beings, the description of such an encounter can often sound gibberish. Many people describe such encounters as a warm, comforting feeling. No matter where they met the angel, they report feeling an immediate sense of well-being. It's almost as if all was right. It can feel like being able to scratch an itch or standing in hot sun. It's more than just a feeling. It's often felt in the bones and deep inside the body. Everyone who has ever told the story of an encounter with an archangel knows the pleasant feeling they had from the first moment that angel arrived.

As the messengers and subjects Gods, it is often the responsibility of the Archangels to bring the Divine blessing to the world. This blessing can heal and is a communication of higher beings. Human convention is too limited to it. While we might not be able see God in person, we can glimpse a small part of his power by interacting with angels. They bring faith and wonder to the whole world.

These encounters may even go unnoticed for some people. It is possible for some people to miss the blessings that are brought into their lives. These moments can give them a profound sense of well-being. It doesn't matter whether the archangels are credited with this healing or not. The archangels have a way of bringing a little more goodness into the world.

We have already spoken extensively about their healing abilities. Their abilities are often discussed in light of the fact that they have not been sent to Earth to make life-altering decisions. Their power is much more subtle than that of prophets and Jesus. They can repair, heal, and mend, but they are not capable of creating. Although they can provide protection in many ways, and it can also be used to heal, repair, and create, it is important that humanity not use the archangels' abilities as a weapon. All who wish to welcome the archangels to their lives should do so with good intentions. The limits of archangels' power are often moral. The archangels' powers are not for selfish, narcissistic, or selfish purposes. They often achieve very little. Those who aim to harm, undercut, or otherwise damage another person are unlikely to succeed. This is simply beyond the capabilities of archangels.

Their potential is far greater than their abilities. It is possible to use faith to bring about amazing results. Combining this knowledge with the healing abilities of the archangels is a powerful combination. It doesn't matter if you are asking for help for a relative who is sick or for protection during difficult times. Anyone with good intentions, the belief in the power and knowledge of the archangels will achieve remarkable results. As you will see, there are specific incantations to attain specific results. This is the end of our discussion on the abstract and philosophical. It can be helpful to review real life examples of people who have accepted archangels in their lives before we proceed.

First-hand accounts on Archangels

The best way to discover more about the nature archangels is to read accounts from those who have interacted with them. These encounters can help us see the truth behind these beings and learn more about their ability to affect our lives. These accounts include those who seek out their guardians and those who are converted to the cause by being randomly blessed. This gives us context to consider how archangels could change our lives.

These pages will feature a few true stories about people who have witnessed the touch and blessings of an archangel. These stories come in many forms, called "angelmedium". This refers to someone who believes that they are able to channel the archangels. Through faith and practice, they are able channel the healing powers and abilities of the Divine beings. It's a fantastic starting point to discuss the phenomenon if you are truly in love with it.

Sarah is the name given to Sarah by the first person. According to Sarah, she received a message through an archangel named Michael. She believed at the time that Michael was spreading His influence all over the world, and that those who believed in his abilities were better positioned to receive his blessing. Sarah was very much in need of his help and his love. Despite being one the busiest and most high ranking archangels, she met Michael when she was in her most desperate hour. This is an example of the reach that angels have when they enter our world.

Sarah is an angel mediator and interacts daily with the Divine spirit. By doing so, Sarah can see the effects they have on the world. Despite her close proximity to the angels, she said that she was surprised to see the effects Michael could have on the quality of her life. It was the lightning fast speed in which the angels responded that she found most impressive. Sarah suggests that this speed is an indication of the angels' genuine care.

The story itself took place in January 1998. Archangel Gabriel Michael had a tremendous impact on Sarah's daily life. On the night of the incident, rain was falling. The storm was intense and the visibility on roads was very poor. It was difficult seeing in any direction. Sarah and her friends decided they were going out to dinner. For several weeks they had planned to visit an Indian place. Even a storm wasn't going to stop them. The restaurant was next to an old railway track. In turn, it was near the docking place for ferries which had since closed down. Sarah and her friends had the task of crossing the railway tracks to reach their destination. The car became stuck when they tried to move it across. Sarah and her 3 friends realized that they were not going anywhere. The car couldn't move.

Sarah got out to investigate the problem. Despite the rain she could see the severity of the problem. The car was solidly stuck to the tracks. There was no way to move it. One of the wheels was raised from the ground and, when the accelerator was pressed it would just spin. Sarah and her friends tried pushing their car. It didn't work. Instead, it just made the car more and more stuck to tracks. The worst problem was Sarah knowing that the train tracks are still in use. Given the poor visibility caused by the storm, there were not many chances that an engineer from the train company would be able see the car in the distance. Sarah had no idea when it might arrive and neither the train engineer nor Sarah knew how they would get the car free. It was stuck completely in place.

Despite having four people present, the car couldn't be lifted from the tracks. Sarah and a friend decided to walk the distance to the restaurant, despite not having any mobile phone technology (it was 1998). Once they reached the restaurant, they could call someone to assist them and try to shift their car before a train arrived. They might still be able get there in time for dinner with some luck. They left behind the two remaining men, who tried to think of other ways to move the vehicle.

Sarah and her friend arrived at the restaurant to call a tow-truck. Sarah thought that while tow truck drivers were usually there to assist with accidents or breakdowns, they might also be able help offer advice. While they managed to reach the restaurant's phones, they could only speak to a recording. Sarah was forced into waiting in line to speak with someone because Sarah couldn't get through to one of the representatives. A train could be arriving at any given moment, so waiting in line over the phone seemed like a terrible idea. Sarah handed the telephone to her friend. She asked her to keep the line open. If the queue were to shorten or the call go through, the friend would be able and willing to explain the situation and to try to quickly dispatch a towtruck to assist them. Sarah started to see the benefits of this idea.

Sarah's mind was flooded with panic and worry up until this moment. It had stopped her thinking clearly. There was only one place she could have gone as an angel mediator. She started to think about Michael's healing abilities and how they might help her. Sarah decided to reach out for help. Sarah was unable to dedicate much time to invocations and the procedures she has grown to love. Instead, she reached out with all of her strength. In a desperate situation she asked Archangel Michael to assist her.

Sarah stepped from the restaurant into pouring rain. Despite the rain, Sarah didn't feel any cold. After only two steps, she could sense a deep warmth in her. Sarah started to get closer to her car and saw the tracks getting more prominent. She could feel movement around the car. The feeling of warmth within her grew, even before she could see the whole vehicle and clearly see every detail. It disappeared as fast as it arrived. Sarah could finally see beyond the clouds, standing in the pouring rain. The car was moving towards Sarah and had gone off the tracks. It circled around Sarah's tracks, drove into the car park and then found a place.

Sarah tried to work out the details. She and her friend went into the restaurant. However, Sarah and the friend were still there to try to figure out what had happened. An additional person had appeared from nowhere. It was one or more of the workers working at the seemingly empty docks. The person saw the car at its halt and offered their assistance. The dockworker, who is a veteran, was able to see how the car became stuck and advise the men what to do. After some effort, the car was finally released from its fateful position thanks to the worker's guidance. Everyone was surprised at the unexpected appearance of the worker. It appeared that he had arrived as Sarah tried to contact him by phone. Sarah realized that the worker had arrived just as Sarah thought she would. The angelic influence of Michael was what she saw in the worker's sudden appearance.

Sarah and her companions went into the restaurant for their planned dinner following the release of the car. After a brief thought, they ventured out into rain, thinking that the ferry worker would come along to eat with them to say thanks. The workers had disappeared just as quickly as they arrived, and it quickly became evident that they had left. Sarah was only able to see the angelic qualities of the worker. When Sarah thought about it later, she realized that the worker was operating under Michael's guidance.

Sarah was to confirm her suspicions later in the evening that Michael was a major influence on the outcome. The group sat down to dinner as the storm continued throughout the night. Sarah was just looking out of the window to observe the weather when she saw a huge flashes of lightning that spread across the sky. This lightning bolt had a special quality. It wasn't the typical white color. This lightning bolt was a deeper blue. Sarah knew that this is the color most associated with Michael the archangel. But that wasn't all. This bolt wasn't the usual fork-shaped shape that lightning takes when moving to the ground. Instead it was shaped like a sword. This weapon is what Archangel Michael often depicts. Sarah believes that this was her guardian angel. It was a confirmation of the fact that he reached down and helped when she needed.

Sarah's doubts concerning archangels, and their power, were completely put to rest by that night. Her strong interactions with the archangels are now a major factor in her angel medium status. Sarah is now a believer in their power, something she had previously known. Sarah says that the events that transpired that night have confirmed her suspicions that the archangels were a reliable and powerful source of goodness for the world. They can be found in all kinds of places.

The next entry will include more than one incident. Sarah was able to confirm her faith. But others can notice an angelic influence in their lives for many years. For many, this is not only a personal revelation but also inspires them and motivates them to help others. Just like this book is written in an effort to welcome others into The Archangel World, others have written down their experiences to help others better understand how complicated the relationship that humans have with the Divine.

This passage will discuss Jane's experiences. Jane has written a whole book detailing her experiences and lessons learned from angels. We will examine one chapter and discuss the lessons we can learn from it. Jane is willing to share the experiences of angel therapy with others even though it might seem a bit strange for some. Michael is the archangel.

Jane confirms that Michael plays a protective and guidance role in Jane's daily life. Jane has been able to trust Michael through the relationships she has with him. He has given her signs of faith to reaffirm the faith she had in the past when she had been doubtful.

Jane considers these signs to be important. Jane views herself as someone who is not willing to commit her life to a single belief. These signs are not always obvious, but they do appear at times when she is awake. They feel like she is feeling something in her stomach. These deep sensations can occur right when Michael is occupying her mind. Alternately, Jane has noticed physical signs that the archangel may be reaching out into her world. This includes one in which a feather drops in such a manner that it touches Jane's area of pain. Jane's daily awareness of Michael in specific places is another way she can be reminded that the angel is always there and able.

Jane recalls when she first learned about the power and existence archangels. Despite having believed in angels in the past, she was skeptical that they would have any influence on her life. Some of the things she learned began to make sense, as she explored the world of the archangels. One of the most striking phenomena that she observed was the existence things that came in threes. These could be numbers, letters or sounds that were repeated 3 times. Jane began to notice how the angels were influencing her whenever such things occurred.

She said that one night she started to drift into sleep. She was almost unconscious when she asked the Archangel Michael for his help. She didn't use any of these traditional invocations. She simply used her growing faith to spread the word throughout the globe. Just before falling asleep she recalls asking the angel for protection and getting a notice that the angel was present in her life. She fell asleep, and it was almost like everything had gone away.

Jane woke before dawn, something that is rare for her on most nights. She still remembers feeling thirsty despite it being dark outside. This was very rare. Jane didn't seem bothered by the situation and walked down a hallway to get water. After returning to her bedroom, Jane found that she was still unable fall asleep. Jane attempted to fall asleep but was unsuccessful so she got up to stand at the window. Jane felt an overwhelming urge to look out at the world instead of just resting on a pillow.

Jane rose and walked to the windows, pulling down the curtains. It was snowing outside as it is every winter. It was February. Jane didn't expect snow to fall that often in her area. Jane loved snow and it was one of the things she enjoyed most about winter. But, the weather was not good enough to convince Jane her prayers were being answered. In fact, she was almost forgetting about the pleas to Michael she sent before she fell asleep. Jane decided to check on the time while she was still awake. Jane reached out for her cellphone and checked the time. It was 3;33 a.m. The clock read three sets of three. She suddenly thought of the many hours she had spent reading books about angels. Jane felt a calm and warm sensation instead of feeling panicked or excited by such a coincidence. Jane took pictures of the snow outside and the time. After getting over her thoughts, she drifted back to sleep.

Jane stepped outside her house to discover that the snow had melted. Jane did not think of the odd events that happened the night before. Jane was pleased to receive a call from husband during her lunch break. After a brief chat she checked her phone to see how many minutes had passed. It took just one minute and eleven second. Another group with three. The numbers were becoming more apparent everywhere. She set aside the thoughts and carried on with her day.

Jane kept a blog. While the blog was strictly personal, Jane loved sharing her thoughts and writing down great deals. People would occasionally comment on the writings she shared with the world after she had shared them. Over the next few days, she visited her blog to check if there was any activity. It was a new visitor who had posted a comment to her blog. Michael. Jane felt a warm glow inside her, smiling at the coincidence. Jane still saw three groups in her daily life. They seemed to be everywhere. Jane acknowledged Michael's message of encouragement and thanked his efforts for making her feel at home.

Jane felt the presence of Michael in her heart over the next weeks. Jane became convinced that these recurring occurrences were the sign her heart desired. Jane can recognize the signs in her life even if she starts doubting an angel's power over her. Jane finds this strength to be a powerful force for good and draws strength from it. Jane finds these signs of archangelic influence or power to be more than enough to show that something greater is possible in the world.

The next case we have comes from someone who has felt a special affinity for angels throughout their life. However, this is not always true. It didn't always happen this way. Joseph, our next entry, is a reflection of twenty years that allows for a lot more hindsight and reflection, which allowed him pinpoint one of the most significant moments in his entire life. Despite being told about God as a kid and the existence of angels when he was a child, it wasn't the events of one single day that led him into believing in the relationship he could have with the Archangels.

Joe was fifteen years-old at the time. This meant that he spent much of his day asleep. Joseph was still asleep during one particular morning. He awoke suddenly and abruptly. He felt that a presence was nearby, but could not pinpoint where and could not see any other person in the room. Although it might have been OK if the spirit had been a positive energy, it felt as though there were negative energies in the room. Joseph could sense the evil force within his bedroom, even though he wasn't aware of it. He became engulfed in panic.

Joseph's mind started to wander back through his childhood as it does for many others in similar situations. The negative presence was growing closer to Joseph and making it difficult for him to move. He remembered something that his sister had taught him as a seven-year-old. He should believe in Archangel Michael should he ever feel devilish forces coming after him. By calling upon the power of angels, he might be capable of drawing the healing strength needed to overcome even the most powerful evil forces.

Joseph, snagged in his bed, thought back to his sister. While it was likely that the time was brief, the next section of his life seemed like it would drag on for minutes to hours. His sister's guidance became more and more apparent to him. With the negative energies growing in strength, there seemed to be no other option. Joseph yelled out into the darkness asking for help from the Archangels. He asked to get saved.

Joseph noticed a flashing, blinding light in his bedroom right away after the words had been spoken. In a split second, Joseph felt the fear and panic that was holding him down to the mattress vanished. This was replaced with a newfound strength. A deafening hum filled his ears. It was almost as if an explosion had struck the room. All was soon back to normal after a mere second. The room was quieted and calm. Joseph opened his eyes. He could see the surrounding area and could see himself lying on the couch. The negative presence had vanished. From that day forward it was gone forever.

www.ingramcontent.com/pod-product-compliance
Lightning Source LLC
Chambersburg PA
CBHW050400120526
44590CB00015B/1768